SOCIAL WORK AND FAITH-BASED ORGANIZATIONS

Faith-based organizations continue to play a significant role in the provision of social work services in many countries but their role within the welfare state is often contested. This text explores their various roles and relationships to social work practice, includes examples from different countries and a range of religious traditions, and identifies challenges and opportunities for the sector.

Social Work and Faith-based Organizations discusses issues such as the relationship between faith-based organizations and the state, working with an organization's stakeholders, ethical practice and dilemmas, and faith-based organizations as employers. It also addresses areas of debate and controversy, such as providing services within and for multi-faith communities and tensions between professional codes of ethics and religious doctrine. Accessibly written by a well-known social work educator, it is illustrated by numerous case studies from a range of countries including Australia, the UK and the US.

Suitable for social work students taking community or administration courses or undertaking placements in faith-based organizations, this innovative book is also a valuable resource for managers and religious personnel who are responsible for the operation of faith-based agencies.

Beth R. Crisp is a Professor in the School of Health and Social Development at Deakin University, Australia where she is the discipline leader for social work.

SOCIAL WORK AND FAITH-BASED ORGANIZATIONS

Beth R. Crisp

Routledge
Taylor & Francis Group

LONDON AND NEW YORK

First published 2014
by Routledge
2 Park Square, Milton Park, Abingdon, Oxon OX14 4RN

and by Routledge
711 Third Avenue, New York, NY 10017

Routledge is an imprint of the Taylor & Francis Group, an informa business

British Library Cataloguing in Publication Data
A catalogue record for this book is available from the British Library

Library of Congress Cataloging-in-Publication Data
Crisp, Beth R.
  Social work and faith-based organizations / Beth R. Crisp.
    pages cm
  ISBN 978-0-415-50980-0 (hardback)—ISBN 978-0-415-50981-7 (pbk.)—
  ISBN 978-1-315-79395-5 (ebook)   1. Faith-based human services.
  2. Social service—Religious aspects.   I. Title.
  HV530.C748 2014
  361.7'5—dc23
                                                    2013040145

ISBN: 978-0-415-50980-0 (hbk)
ISBN: 978-0-415-50981-7 (pbk)
ISBN: 978-1-315-79395-5 (ebk)

Typeset in Sabon
by Keystroke, Station Road, Codsall, Wolverhampton

Printed and bound in the United States of America by
Edwards Brothers Malloy

CONTENTS

INTRODUCTION

Until a few decades ago and similar to many other countries, most welfare services in Australia were funded and conducted by religious organizations to service the needs of co-religionists. Yet despite the emergence of the welfare state and changes in patterns of religious belief, faith-based welfare organizations continue to flourish and make a major contribution to the well-being of Australians. However, any assumptions of previous generations about faith-based organizations no longer hold. Most are very different from their predecessors, many receiving much, if not all, their funding from the state, professional staff are often not co-religionists and may not have any religious beliefs, and services are provided to all members of the community irrespective of their religious beliefs. Furthermore, their role is often contested, and many faith-based organizations are themselves engaging in discussions as to what it means to be a faith-based provider of services in the twenty-first century (Crisp 2010).

It is perhaps inevitable that such questions are being asked in Australia, where non-government (voluntary) organizations provide at least half of all welfare services, and faith-based services have been central to this provision (Melville and McDonald 2006; Swain 2009). A 2006 survey by *Business Review Weekly* identified 23 of the top 25 Australian charities in terms of annual income as being associated with Christian churches (Lake 2013), several of which employ hundreds of staff (Holden and Trembath 2008) and are among the largest employers of qualified social workers (Camilleri and Winkworth 2004).

Although some of the questions being asked in Australia about the role of faith-based organizations relate to specific issues within Australia, questions about the role of faith-based organizations in welfare provision are being asked in many countries (e.g. Bäckström *et al.* 2010, 2011; Ellenson 2006;

Göcmen 2013; Jeppsson Grassman 2010; Vanderwoerd 2004). This is perhaps unsurprising given estimates that 90 per cent of the global humanitarian workforce work from a faith basis, and the majority of agencies they work for are faith based (Ager and Ager 2011). As part of a larger trend which recognizes that the place of religion in society can no longer be ignored as many tried to do in the twentieth century (Campbell 2009; Gray *et al.* 2009), the early years of the twenty-first century have seen renewed interest in the role of faith-based organizations in the social services at policy level with governments in a number of countries, including Australia (Ayton *et al.* 2012; Holden and Trembath 2008), the United Kingdom (Harris *et al.* 2003), the United States (Unruh and Sider 2005), Canada (Hiemstra 2002) and New Zealand (Milligan and Conradson 2011), proposing that churches and religious agencies take more responsibility for provision of welfare services. For example, the UK government's emphasis on the 'Big Society' proposes that community groups, including faith-based agencies, are valuable to society (Dinham 2012a), and assumes that they are able and willing to take on a greater role in the provision of social services (Furness and Gilligan 2012). At the same time, there has been considerable scepticism as to the appropriateness of faith-based organizations providing welfare services in multi-faith communities, as well as allegations of sexual and other forms of abuse which are revealing some faith-based organizations as being significantly flawed and engaging in unethical practices.

The contemporary debates as to the role of faith-based organizations in welfare provision are highlighting a relative lack of serious consideration of the relationship between faith-based organizations and social work practice which was almost non-existent prior to the 1990s (Horsburgh 1988). In the late 1990s in the UK, Bowpitt commented that the historical role of religious organizations in welfare provision was often regarded as a 'legacy [which] has been the skeleton in the cupboard, something best forgotten and preferably ignored' (Bowpitt 1998: 676). Around the same time, Cnaan *et al.*, writing in North America, noted:

> Unfashionable and unpopular as this may be in social work circles, we believe it is essential that the role of religious-based organizations in welfare provision be addressed because of its significance for the directions that provision of social services will take in the years ahead.
> (Cnaan *et al.* 1999: xi)

That churches and church-connected groups should be involved in welfare provision was largely unquestioned in the nineteenth and early part of the twentieth century (Holden and Trembath 2008), with the exception of the motivations of a few very evangelical groups (Swain 2005). However, there has been much more debate in recent years concerning the religious content of programmes or the religious beliefs of practitioners or service users than about the role of faith-based organizations as providers of professional social work services (Cnaan *et al.* 1999; Sherr and Rogers 2009). Often this has been highly critical:

> Social work authors sometimes report a distorted view of the profession's entire history . . . with no mention of the contributions of early church-related agencies. . . . If church affiliated agencies are mentioned at all, they may be portrayed as over-zealous or incompetent meddlers operating poorly-run agencies.
>
> (Scales 2011: 353)

Contemporary textbooks on human services provision used by social work students may make passing references to faith-based organizations but lack a critical discussion about this sector's role in welfare provision (e.g. Gardner 2006; Ozanne and Rose 2013). Similarly, the lack of attention to religious antecedents of welfare policy has been noted in respect of textbooks for social policy students (Jawad 2012b). However, before considering what the role of faith-based social work provision is or could be, the considerable efforts which have occurred in many places to rewrite social work history with a view to removing traces of the contribution of religious groups or organizations must be recognized. For example, in Australia, the pivotal role religious groups played in the development of professional social work is better appreciated by welfare historians than by contemporary social workers (Gleeson 2008a). In 1928, the Catholic Church sponsored scholarships for two students to undertake social work training at the Catholic University of America, who on their return were credited as being Australia's first trained social workers (Gleeson 2000). Welfare agencies under the auspices of churches were the first non-government organizations to employ professional social workers (Holden and Trembath 2008) and to insist that government-funded counselling programmes were staffed by qualified social workers (Gleeson 2008b).

While it is recognized that many churches and other religious organizations provide forms of welfare or social assistance to individuals in need, the focus of this book concerns the subset of welfare work provided by faith-based organizations which is undertaken by professionally qualified social workers. This is in contrast with recent research about welfare provision by churches in Europe, where it is not uncommon to see the term 'social work' used in respect of a wide range of care roles provided by the church and not necessarily confined to the work of professional social workers (Middlemiss 2006a; Yeung 2006).

The approach adopted in this book involved inductive exploratory research starting with the questions 'What is the nature scope of professional social work practice in faith-based organizations?' and 'What difference does it make to the practice experience for social workers employed in faith-based organizations?' Given that the role of faith-based organizations in the provision of social welfare differs between countries (Ferguson 2004), it has been necessary to acknowledge Payne's (2005) concern in terms of not adopting an internationalist perspective which homogenizes the experiences in different countries, but nevertheless recognizing that many of the issues cross national borders. It was also necessary to acknowledge that although much of the most accessible literature concerning social work practice in faith-based organizations has emerged from the US (Schwartz *et al.* 2008), theorizing about faith-based organizations emerging from US research does not readily apply in other countries (Schneider 2013). Furthermore, US research has not necessarily addressed the questions which are being asked elsewhere (Swain 2005). In recent years the key emphasis of much of the US research has been on efficacy and outcomes of publicly funded programmes (Torry 2005) rather than the more philosophical questions which led to this research. Yet even within the US, the dominance of this emphasis has been problematic:

> Current social work research on religious organizations is problematic in that studies focus primarily on evaluation of outcomes and not enough on understanding the unique contexts of religious organizations as human service providers.
>
> (Yancey *et al.* 2009: 131)

When asked to compare research from the US and UK in the area of spirituality and mental health, Swinton (2007) concluded that much of the US research was concerned with religious participation and the function or health benefits of religion and spirituality for individuals. In contrast, much of the UK research was concerned with concepts, the meaning of the care provided for service users and practice issues associated with providing spiritual care. As such, he noted:

> There is therefore an interesting difference in approach and style with UK-based studies tending to focus on research that is primarily aimed at practice which, at times reacts strongly against the methods and assumptions of science, and the US where the emphasis is on credibility and importance of science for helping us to understand the health benefits of religion.
>
> (Swinton 2007: 302)

By intentionally seeking out and reviewing relevant literature from a wide range of countries, there was an expectation that this might lead to new questions or perspectives about faith-based organizations. As social work services are provided in many countries by international aid and relief agencies, many of which work from a faith basis (De Cordier 2009), in addition to the more traditional social work canon, relevant literature on the role of faith-based organizations in international aid and development was also considered relevant to this project (Jawad 2012b).

Although providing a wide range of fascinating insights into welfare provision by faith-based organizations, the existing literature left several questions unanswered, particularly in respect of the practice experiences of professional social workers. In order to explore some of these emerging questions, semi-structured interviews were undertaken between November 2011 and October 2012 with 20 social workers in the state of Victoria in Australia who were currently, or had previously been employed in a faith-based organization. A further five interviews were conducted with social workers in Scotland in May and June 2013 who had social work practice experience in a faith-based organization. The many quotes appearing in this book which have no citation are from this interview data.

In interviews lasting between 20 minutes and one hour, participants were asked questions such as 'What is the role of faith-based welfare organizations in a multi-faith society?', 'Why do/did you work for a faith-based organization?', 'How different, if at all, is it working for a faith-based agency than for another type of agency?', 'Are there any tensions between the religious beliefs or values espoused by the organization and your understanding of social work?' and 'What do you see as the future prospects and challenges for faith-based agencies?' Ethical approval was obtained from the Health Ethics Committee at Deakin University.

With the consent of participants, the interviews were audio-recorded. Transcribed interviews were sent to participants for their review and any changes were included in the transcripts which were subjected to thematic analysis. Recognizing the considerable diversity among faith-based organizations providing social work services (Yancey *et al.* 2009), thematic analysis was undertaken, as this is an inductive technique which facilitates identification of a diverse range of experiences rather than seeking to deductively categorize information in accordance with a pre-existing schema.

As others researching in this field have found, anonymity in respect of both themselves and the organizations in which they were currently or had previously been employed was a particular concern to several of the research participants (Dinham 2012a). In response to these concerns, and in recognition that although the content of an individual quote might not identify an individual, multiple pieces of information attributed to the same individual might well reveal details which could potentially facilitate identification of individuals or organizations. Hence quotes or other information from individual research participants are un-ascribed in order to retain anonymity. Although many of the reflections and experiences of the Australian and Scottish social workers were not dissimilar, where there seemed to be considerable differences between the Australian and Scottish experience, comments by individual research participants will be delineated by country.

Preserving anonymity has in some instances required adopting generic language which is sufficiently descriptive to enable sense to be made of information but without risking identification of a religion or organization. Designations which may be specific to particular religious groups include the job titles of church workers (Middlemiss 2006a) and organizational structures such as 'diocese', 'province', 'territory' or 'presbytery'. Conversely, religious language may often have different meanings according to the specific religious context. For example, the designation of a religious official as 'bishop' may mean quite different roles in different religions (Ekstrand 2011), as may 'congregation' (Torry 2005).

The research participants ranged from relatively new graduates in their first position since qualifying as a social worker, to middle-level managers and chief executives. Although all held a social work qualification and considered themselves to be social workers, many participants in both countries had job titles other than 'social worker'. In Scotland participants included both those who held positions which are restricted to registered social workers and those working in positions which are not classified as social work positions by the registration authority. As one Scottish social worker explained:

> Well, yes there's some people, they may have trained as social workers, but because they wanted to work for the organization they got a job there, so they just are – most of the staff positions are either 'support worker' or 'project worker'.

The key focus of participants' work included case work, counselling, community development, policy work, research and management. The fields of practice in which they worked included adoption and fostering, aged care, children and families, drug and alcohol services, juvenile justice, mental health, relationship counselling and school social work. Although there were no restrictions on the type of work, field of practice, level of experience or religious beliefs held by participants, to facilitate a diversity of experiences it was determined that a maximum of three research participants be recruited from any single organization.

While participants were sought from a wide range of faith-based welfare organizations in both Victoria and Scotland, attempts to recruit participants were most successful in organizations where the author or her colleagues had existing relationships, or when participants recommended colleagues who they thought might be interested in engaging with the interview questions. Consequently, only two Australian participants and none of the Scottish participants had been employed in organizations associated with non-Christian religions. On the other hand, the organizations represented in this study are generally representative of the faith-based welfare sector in Australia (Swain 2009) and Scotland (Cree 1996).

As with any research, the methodology has its limitations, and a key limitation of this project has been the dominance of experiences associated with Christianity. Even when researchers make efforts to recruit participants beyond mainstream religious groups, welfare organizations associated with other religions may decline to participate (Edwards 2013). As others have found, locating social workers in faith-based organizations requires considerable effort (Cnaan *et al.* 1999; Dinham 2009). Although there are some large and well-known faith-based welfare organizations in both Victoria and Scotland, full listings of such organizations which employ social workers do not exist, as small faith-based welfare initiatives are not always well known, even by the broader human services networks (Grønbjerg and Nelson 1998). Furthermore, organizations which one would surmise might employ social workers don't necessarily do so (Northern 2009; Schwartz *et al.* 2008). While acknowledging these limitations, it is nevertheless hoped that some of the ideas and insights which are raised may stimulate further thinking and research into faith-based social work practice in other contexts, and contribute to an ongoing international dialogue.

Chapter 1 explores the question of just what is meant by the term 'faith-based organization'. This chapter establishes that there is no universally accepted definition as to what is a faith-based organization and explores a range of criteria which may be used for determining whether or not an organization may be considered 'faith based'. While accepting that this is contestable, a working definition of 'faith-based organization' is nevertheless provided for the purposes of this book.

Having defined what a faith-based organization is, Chapter 2 turns to exploring the relationship between faith-based organizations and the contemporary welfare state which has been subject to considerable debate since the middle of the twentieth century. While there are some who consider that the emergence of the secular welfare state has left little or no need for faith-based organizations, faith-based organizations can work in partnership with the state to be provide essential welfare services to individuals and communities, and/or they may play key roles in advocacy and developing social policy.

The question of the role of faith-based organizations in a multi-faith society is then considered in Chapter 3. Faith-based organizations may have been originally established to meet the needs of a particular religious constituency but changing circumstances can result in questions being asked as to whether it is appropriate for them to be providing services to the wider community. This is particularly the case in fields of practice where faith-based organizations often have considerable expertise such as in provision of care to immigrants, including refugees and asylum seekers.

Chapter 4 identifies a range of stakeholder groups in the work of faith-based organizations, each of which may have their own perspectives and issues. These include the religious communities which have supported the initial development and ongoing work of faith-based initiatives, the professional community, including social workers who are employed in faith-based organizations, service users, funders, the wider community and the board of management. In particular, this chapter will consider the inherent tensions which can emerge among stakeholders with diverse interests.

Faith-based organizations are considered to be a desirable workplace by some social workers. Hence, Chapter 5 explores the employment experience for social workers in faith-based organizations and identifies reasons why this can be an attractive employment option as well as some issues in working conditions.

Chapter 6 explores the issue of ethical social work practice in faith-based agencies. For professional social workers, there may be the potential for tension if the religious values underpinning the organization collide with professional codes of ethics. This chapter also considers the issue of what is ethical practice for a faith-based organization when confronted with legislative requirements for practice which are seemingly in conflict with religious values.

While there is little doubt that many contemporary faith-based organizations are committed to providing services which conform with best practice principles, some faith-based organizations have been forced to recognize that they have engaged in practices that have been denounced. Chapter 7 explores the issue of controversies associated with faith-based organizations. Scandals involving physical, mental and sexual abuse of children in their care have highlighted both the high expectations in which societies hold faith-based agencies and some histories of deeply problematical agency practices. This chapter explores what may be learned from the histories of these organizations and the challenges they present for contemporary social work practice.

Finally, Chapter 8 draws together the key ideas presented in the preceding chapters and identifies some prospects and challenges for faith-based social work provision.

The writing of this book was made possible by Deakin University in the form of a period of academic study leave and a travel grant which enabled me to spend several months in 2013 undertaking research in the United Kingdom. Additional funding and a visiting fellowship with The Institute for the Advanced Studies in the Humanities (IASH) and the School of Social and Political Studies (SSPS) at the University of Edinburgh ensured that I had a genial and creative environment in which to work. At IASH I enjoyed frequent stimulating encounters with other visiting scholars in fields far beyond the imagination of a scholar normally based in a Faculty of Health and I am grateful to the IASH staff, particularly Professor Jolyon Mitchell and Anthea Taylor, for curating a programme of seminars and social activities which were both intellectually energizing and most enjoyable. In SSPS, several staff members offered advice as I sought to undertake field research in Scotland, and Professor Viviene Cree and Dr Mark Smith in particular provided sounding-boards as I attempted to make sense of the place of faith-based organizations in the Scottish context. As well as the necessary infrastructure support, including library and IT access, members of Deakin and Edinburgh universities provided much feedback and made valuable suggestions both at public seminars and in individual conversations. Prior to returning to Deakin, I was also able to take up a scholarship to work in Gladstone's Library in North Wales which also proved to be a stimulating and encouraging environment in which to write.

Many individuals in faith-based organizations in both Victoria and Scotland have supported this project. Most notable are the 25 social workers who took time out from their schedules to be interviewed and were frequently disarmingly frank in discussing their working lives in faith-based organizations. Some participants also assisted in recruiting further interviewees, and there were also non-social work staff members in some organizations who provided details of the study to their social work qualified colleagues. Once again I am grateful to a number of friends and colleagues, including Professor Viviene Cree, Professor Michael Ross and Mark Anderson, for finding the time to provide critical feedback on drafts of the manuscript.

Finally, as always, Mark Anderson is incredibly generous in his support of my writing projects, but even more is his constant support for me through all the trials and tribulations of life, and particularly as we negotiated our way through the aftermath of two family deaths during this project. This book is dedicated to him.

1

WHAT ARE FAITH-BASED ORGANIZATIONS?

With non-governmental actors increasingly enmeshed within inter-governmental structures and governmental agendas, the principles and policies of humanitarianism were increasingly articulated in secular terms. Organizations with varying connections to faith traditions generally adopted an approach and discourse that rendered it difficult to distinguish them on many criteria from secular agencies.

(Ager and Ager 2011: 457)

Introduction

It has been proposed that 'welfare services constitute a site where the sacred and secular interact' (Angell 2010: 75) but, as the above quote suggests, just what distinguishes a so-called 'faith-based organization' from other services may not be readily apparent. Nor is there any consensus as to what the term 'faith-based organization' means (Hugen and Venema 2009), or even whether it is an appropriate term to describe initiatives of religious groups for whom 'faith' is not a key component of their religion (Alison 2010). That 'faith' is often regarded as synonymous with religion reflects the overwhelming influence of Christianity, Islam and Judaism in the literature about welfare provision by religious organizations, and a lack of recognition that 'faith' is not necessarily the most important tenet in some other religions. But some have proposed that the focus on 'faith' reflects a predominantly Protestant and Western perspective in the literature (e.g. Jawad 2009). Hence, it is important to clarify at the outset that in using the term 'faith-based organization', this book is referring to a social service agency which employs qualified social workers and has its 'identity and mission . . . self-consciously derived from the teachings of one or more religious or spiritual traditions' (Berger 2003: 16) and/or is auspiced by any religious organization or religious community (Palmer 2011). In addition to welfare organizations established by religious organizations, in some countries there is also a tradition of philanthropic organizations established by the urban bourgeoisie or nobility which take their inspiration from, and identify with, religious teachings (Fix and Fix 2002). Hence, the definition of faith-based organization which has been adopted in this book is 'a social service agency which explicitly identifies with a religious tradition and/or is auspiced by any religious organization or religious community or organization. Programmes or services offered by a faith-based agency don't necessarily have any religious content.'

Like Jeavons (2004), this book has restricted the scope further to organizations which employ qualified social workers, but recognizes that this is a narrower definition than has sometimes been adopted by those writing about faith-based organizations (e.g. McGrew and Cnaan 2006), who will sometimes refer to 'any kind of faith-related voluntary association (including churches, mosques, synagogues, and congregations) engaging in social welfare' (Göcmen 2013: 496). Such a broad definition includes organizations where welfare provision is not among their key reasons for existence (Unruh and Sider 2005).

Expressions of faith include the branding of an organization, organizational structure, how it understands its purpose, and the role of religion in service provision (Cnaan and Boddie 2006; Unruh and Sider 2005). Each of these expressions will now be considered in turn, along with the impact of changing circumstances upon the faith basis of welfare organizations.

Branding

The branding of an organization, including the name and signage, are often the first indications that it may have some faith basis, but this is not necessarily an accurate predictor, with some faith-based organizations intentionally choosing names which have no religious connotations (Ebaugh *et al.* 2003). For example, in New York a faith-based organization serving people with HIV/AIDS changed its name from 'Upper Room' to 'Harlem United', downplaying its religious basis and seeking to emphasize the compassionate and non-judgemental nature of the services provided (Chambre 2001). On the other hand, having a name with religious connotations may be more a reflection of history than of contemporary circumstances. Although its name and symbol might suggest a religious organization, the Red Cross is typically now regarded to be an organization which had religious origins but which is now ostensibly secular (Cnaan *et al.* 1999).

An analysis of the names of the approximately 50 publicly listed member organizations of Catholic Social Services Victoria (2013) reveals considerable diversity in naming, even by organizations which are all associated with one religion in one Australian state. Member organizations had names which could be categorized as follows:

- Explicitly Catholic (e.g. CatholicCare).
- Obviously Catholic to anyone who knows some basics about Catholic culture (e.g. Corpus Christi Community).
- Obviously Catholic to those with some advanced knowledge about Catholicism (e.g. Edmund Rice Camps, MacKillop Family Services).
- Of some religious persuasion (e.g. Bethlehem Community Inc.).
- Of no obvious religious persuasion (e.g. Keysborough Learning Centre, Griefline).

The importance of the name was discussed by a number of the Australian research participants, particularly in respect of many of the welfare agencies associated with Roman Catholic dioceses across the country changing their name from 'Centacare' to the more ostensibly religious 'Catholic-Care' which was commented on by social workers working for other organizations. One explanation given to the author was that this name change was premised on a belief that this would endear the agencies more to the Catholic community by being more upfront as to this being a church response to the welfare needs in the community. Observations from Australian social workers in Catholic welfare organizations included the comment:

> [I]n our diocese, they think parishioners don't see Centacare as Catholic, you know, as a response from the church to welfare. So they think the name, if you call it CatholicCare, people when they see CatholicCare in the paper will think here is the church doing something good.

However, concerns were also raised that this might alienate potential service users and it was observed that such changes may be more about serving the needs of the religious faithful than in affecting how services are provided.

A further complication with naming is that some external programme funding requires host organizations to promote the name of the programme rather than of the auspicing organization. This may include using programme rather than agency letterhead, such that service users may be quite unaware that the services they are receiving are actually being provided by a faith-based organization.

Acknowledging that the distinction between religious and cultural symbols can be blurred (Netting 2004), visual branding may nevertheless also be used to promote messages as to the extent to which an organization is faith based (Ebaugh *et al.* 2003). In an organization where some research participants actually questioned whether or not it was really 'faith based', it was noted that the symbol of the cross on the logo, once prominent, had become much less noticeable on a recent revision. This does not necessarily reflect any lessening of religious faith in the organization's underpinnings or values but may represent a conscious decision that their faith is best expressed in how they treat service users rather than in the use of symbols or signage (Tangenberg 2005).

How organizations brand themselves is not only important in respect of communications with service users, but also to other stakeholders including donors. In an analysis of religious welfare organizations in Lebanon, it was observed that whereas some organizations appealed to donors on the basis of being a 'civilizing force', others marketed donations as being a form of religious 'worship' (Jawad 2009: 109). However, despite what may seem apparent branding as being faith based, organizations may not be recognized as such in the wider community (Jawad 2012b). For example, in the UK, the Charity Commission for England and Wales does not necessarily classify welfare organizations as having a faith basis, even though this might be implicit in their name, such as Jewish Care. Only organizations which explicitly state their objectives as religious rather than welfare provision are readily identifiable as having a faith basis (Charities Aid Foundation 2013).

Organizational structures

Whether or not indicated in their name, faith-based organizations typically have some degree of affiliation with a religious constituency, and it is this religious affiliation that differentiates them from their secular counterparts (Ferris 2005). This may include welfare services auspiced by local groups or congregations, those at the district or diocesan level, and independent welfare organizations that are affiliated with one or more faith communities (Leis-Peters 2006, 2010; Sinha 2013). Furthermore, there are organizations with a faith basis which may operate independently of institutional religion and have only informal connections with religious hierarchies (Deines 2008), although they may have had such relationships previously (Davis *et al.* 2008).

Both national and religious characteristics may influence the organization of faith-based welfare services. Over the past decade and a half, much of the literature which has emerged concerning faith-based welfare provision and which has originated from the US has focused on initiatives provided by local faith congregations (e.g. Boddie and Cnaan 2006; Tirrito and Cascio 2003), particularly from those associated with Pro-testant forms of Christianity (Unruh and Sider 2005). However, some religions (e.g. Catholicism and Judaism) have more of a propensity to develop centralized services which may be organized on a national or regional (e.g. state, province, diocese) basis (Sinha 2013). Such services, although often underpinned by religious teachings, are about a need for taking communal responsibility for members of society experiencing disadvantage, rather than an explicit faith-based identity (Wittberg 2013). Hence, within a nation such as the US, it has been proposed that models for analysing Protestant faith-based initiatives may have limited utility in other settings (Jeavons 2004; Smith and Sosin 2001).

In contrast to the US, Australian faith-based welfare organizations are often associated with religions which have strong national or international structures, resulting in welfare agencies often being organized at regional or diocesan level (Himchak 2005). Particularly since the mid-1990s, but to some extent before then, the welfare agencies of the major Christian churches in Australia have formed alliances with similar agencies from either the same or from other regions. This has led to the establishment of some large organizations under a single management structure, agencies such as CatholicCare, Anglicare and UnitingCare, which are national federations of locally run welfare organizations associated with the country's three largest religious groups. Nevertheless, this trend of federating welfare organizations associated with a particular religion under a single umbrella is not confined to Australia and has also occurred in the US (Vanderwoerd 2004).

A key aspect of organizational structures concerns decision-making processes within organizations. It may be important that the leadership is both skilled in managing a welfare agency and that there are processes reflecting the religious beliefs of the religious auspice (Schneider 1999). Whereas in some faith-based welfare organizations the major decisions are made by management groups controlled by the religious auspice, in others, the auspicing group (or groups) may be entitled to nominate some but not all members of a board of management. Furthermore, there may be rules as to how many, if not all, board members are required to be co-religionists (Holden and Trembath 2008; Sinha 2013).

A mix of motivations for appointments to a board of management of a faith-based organization can readily lead to decision-making in faith-based organizations which is at least in part based on maintaining ethics or values rather than purely rational grounds (Torry 2005). Hence, Clarke and Jennings (2008) have proposed that the term 'faith-based organization' refer to 'any organization that derives inspiration and guidance for its activities from the teachings and principles of the faith or from a particular interpretation or school of thought within the faith' (Clarke and Jennings 2008: 6). But just because people claim to believe in God or some other deity does not necessarily result in a consensus as to what this means, and the implications for service provision (Dezerotes 2009).

While some may argue that this is no more than wishful thinking, it has been declared that:

> Faith-based organizations have a set of characteristics that distinguish them from their secular counterparts. The language of faith, the religious idiom, frequently better reflects the cultural norms in which the poor and marginalized operate.
>
> (Clarke and Jennings 2008: 15)

Alternatively, faith-based organizations may reflect the cultural norms of the groups which established them. For example, in Lebanon five types of religious welfare organizations have been identified: organizations established and managed by religious orders, charitable organizations set up by elite families associated with a religious tradition, religious organizations associated with popular political movements, international humanitarian relief organizations, and religious organizations closely associated with the state. Not only are these organizations distinguishable in terms of organizational structure, but also in terms of their aims or mission (Jawad 2009).

Purpose

Although faith-based organizations are those that derive their identity and purpose from a particular religious or spiritual tradition (Berger 2003; Palmer 2011), organizations which emerge from the same religious tradition may develop divergent understandings as to what their purpose should be (Cameron 2004). For example, Catholic social teaching has been regarded as 'the most systematic and thorough attempt by a religious faith to articulate its position on social policy' (Brenden 2007: 477), and frequently informs understandings of social responsibility and welfare provision in other Christian traditions (Campbell 2012), but can lead to radically different outcomes depending on how it is interpreted. However, although both justice for the individual and in society are recognized, interpretations of Catholic social teaching often give preference to one or other of these emphases (Campbell 2012).

Some religious organizations have understood their purpose in the wider world to consist of providing services to disadvantaged members of the community with little or no expectation of altering the religious beliefs and practices of those to whom the services are provided (Davies-Kildea 2007). To guard against accusations of proselytizing, some faith-based organizations make it known to staff that they may face being dismissed from their position if they seek to convert service users (Conradson 2011), while in others staff are encouraged to change the topic when service users raise issues of a religious or spiritual nature (Pipes and Ebaugh 2002). Elsewhere, however, the hope of religious conversion underpins service provision by some religious organizations (De Cordier 2009). This can range from low-key invitations about which the recipient is made aware that their decision to participate or not in religious activities will have no impact on receipt of welfare services, through to coercive or manipulative attempts involving inducements for those who choose to become involved in a religion (Battin 1990), including providing services only to individuals who have participated in religious activities such as prayers or worship conducted by the organization (Belcher and DeForge 2007). Hence, Gilligan (2010: 61) has identified two contrasting approaches to faith-based social work which he has labelled 'liberal or open' and 'fundamentalist or exclusive'. In the former approach religious beliefs are recognized as an underlying motivation to service provision and the religious underpinnings of a programme or agency may in fact emerge in the public sphere as a commitment to 'care' (e.g. Belcher 2008; Camilleri and Winkworth 2005; Conradson 2011) rather than use explicitly religious language, whereas the latter is premised on the belief that religious salvation is the ultimate imperative (Scales 2011).

This question is whether faith-based welfare organizations are called to be the 'mouthpiece of God' or 'the quiet voice of God' (Pessi 2010: 88); in other words, are they called to preach or to be a presence through service provision? This is far from a new question, and in her analysis of late nineteenth-century welfare services in Australia, Swain has reported:

> A far more influential factor in the structuring of faith-based welfare services was the distinction between Evangelical and incarnational understandings of the Christian duty and service. Confident in their own forgiveness, Evangelicals ranging from Anglicans through to Salvationists, became involved in charity as a way of bringing people to God. Consequently, they measured their success in terms of conversions gained rather than poverty relieved. Their good works served as a demonstration of individual conversion, fulfilling their duty as Christians to show love for others. Because they understood poverty to be a result of sinfulness, Evangelicals offered forgiveness rather than condemnation, and preferred to see the institutions they established as 'homes' rather than asylums of reformatories. However, their compassion was tempered by a sense of moral superiority, which justified their interference in the lives of those who came to them for help. . . . Catholics and Anglo-Catholics took a more incarnational view, valuing the poor because their suffering was seen as bringing them closer to God. Charity was not primarily about evangelisation, but about bearing witness and adhering to the values of the Gospel, seeing the Christ rather than the sinners in the individual who came to them for help. In their churches and institutions, they looked for outward conformity rather than individual conversion, believing that ritual and practice would bring the poor to salvation.
>
> (Swain 2009: 689–690)

Payne (2005) paints a similar story in Britain in the nineteenth century where the evangelicals were most likely to regard themselves as successful if they achieved conversion. Such tensions were also being played out in the US where some early leaders in the Charity Organization Societies warned volunteers that the aim of 'friendly visiting' was not spiritual conversion but rather to provide charity to the most needy and vulnerable members of the community (Scales and Kelly 2011).

Clarke's (2008) writing on the role of faith-based organizations in development studies has proposed that, rather than a dichotomy between implicit and explicit expressions of religion, a continuum is required. In particular, he notes four main ways in which faith manifests itself in the work of faith-based organizations:

> *Passive*: The teachings of the faith (or sub-faith) are subsidiary to broader humanitarian principles as a motivation for action and in mobilizing staff and supporters and play a secondary role to humanitarian considerations in identifying, helping or working with beneficiaries and partners.
>
> *Active*: Faith provides an important and explicit motivation for action and in mobilizing staff and supporters. It plays a direct role in identifying, helping or working with beneficiaries and partners, although there is no overt discrimination against non-believers and the organization supports multi-faith cooperation.
>
> *Persuasive*: Faith provides an important and explicit motivation for action and in mobilizing staff and supporters. It plays a significant role in identifying, helping or working with beneficiaries and partners and provides the dominant basis for engagement. It aims to bring new converts to the faith (or a particular branch of the faith) and/or to advance the interests of the faith/sub-faith at the expense of others.
>
> *Exclusive*: Faith provides the principal or overriding motivation for action and in mobilizing staff and supporters. It provides the principal or sole consideration in identifying beneficiaries. Social and political engagement is rooted in the faith, or a branch of the faith, and is often militant or violent, and/or directed against one or more rival faiths.
>
> (Clarke 2008: 32–33)

Clarke notes that it is the first and second categories of faith-based organizations that are most likely to attract support, including financial donations, in the wider community. Furthermore, such organizations may truly believe that addressing humanitarian concerns is more urgent than addressing religious practice. For example, Islamic Relief in Bangladesh acknowledged that the facilities for community prayer available in a refugee camp were inappropriate but considered its priorities to be concerned around ensuring basic living standards in terms of food, shelter, water and sanitation (Palmer 2011). Nevertheless, potentially all four of Clarke's organizational categories allow for faith-based organizations to be 'prophetic' (Campbell 2012: 101) and 'to care for the vulnerable' (Campbell 2012: 102). Moreover, although explicitly religious outcomes are only mentioned in the latter two of Clarke's categories, to some extent these may also underpin the expectations of stakeholders in the first two categories (Fischer and Stelter 2006).

While conversion is often considered in respect of non-members becoming active in, and taking on the values of, a new religion, an expectation of conversion may also be placed upon members whose beliefs or actions are considered to be in opposition to religious teachings (Battin 1990). For example, Islamic charities in Somalia often seek to create 'good' Muslims who will 'purify their practice' (Kroessin and Mohamed 2008: 207) rather than win new converts to Islam. An example of this may also be found in Melbourne, Australia, where the message of an education campaign aimed at Muslim men was that 'Violence against women is illegal and betrays the example set by our Prophet'.

Whether faith-based organizations view their purpose as predominantly serving co-religionists or outsiders is also critical (Thyer 2006), given that services provided by religious agencies to members of their own religion may vary considerably from services aimed at the wider community (Baker 2012). For instance, faith-based welfare organizations, particularly those associated with immigrant groups, will often provide services only to their own community members (Clarke 2008) and, in turn, may be preferred by members of their communities for their ability to provide culturally and/or linguistically sensitive services (Boddie *et al.* 2011; Lovat 2010). Furthermore, organizations associated with minority religions are often concerned to pass their faith on to their youth, which is not only an investment by religious organizations in the long-term future of their communities, but also because this contributes to civil society more generally by being a moderating influence against extremism (Green 2010).

Seeking to understand the purpose of a faith-based organization requires going beyond focusing on the attributes of the organization and taking account of expected service user characteristics, particularly in respect of their religious beliefs or affiliations. Whether recipients of welfare services are viewed primarily as service users or as potential converts will affect both how services are provided and the service user experience (Grønbjerg and Nelson 1998). Figure 1.1 proposes a new way of considering faith-based organizations which takes account of both of these dimensions.

Figure 1.1 consists of two intersecting continua. The first of these continua relates to the target group, and whether it is exclusively or primarily aimed at members or non-members of a religious community. This crosses a continuum in which the explicit emphasis of service provision

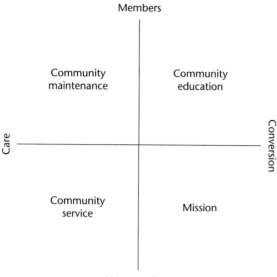

FIGURE 1.1   Service orientation of faith-based organizations as determined by target group (members versus non-members) and service aim (care versus conversion)

varies, ranging from being primarily concerned with care to a strong emphasis on conversion.

The emphasis of organizations which primarily provide care services for members of a faith community may be typified as **community maintenance**. An example of this would be the welfare programmes of the Church of Sweden. With the majority of Swedes identifying as members of the Church of Sweden, the welfare work of the Church is primarily to its own members (Crisp 2013). But given that religion is widely regarded to be a private matter in Swedish society (Edgardh Beckman *et al.* 2006), services provided by the Church of Sweden place their emphasis on care rather than on religious conversion. Similarly, many Jewish welfare organizations tend to provide services largely to their own members, and actively seeking converts is not a feature of Judaism.

In contrast to the Church of Sweden, services provided by welfare organizations associated with the Catholic Church in Australia which are often aimed at the wider community (Crisp 2013) tend to be characterized by an ethic of **community service**. As might be expected in settings which are staffed by welfare professionals (Smith and Sosin 2001), religious conversion is not considered a primary aim of welfare provision in programmes characterized by community service.

Services aimed at community members which place an emphasis on religious conversion will have a **community education** focus. An example of this is the domestic violence prevention programme mentioned previously which appeals to the religious beliefs of Islamic men.

The fourth quadrant which comprises organizations and programmes aimed at non-community members with a strong religious focus may be typified as **mission**. Staff are typically required to be of the faith and programmes have a strong religious content. Many faith-based welfare programmes offered in the US which include explicit religious content may be characterized in this quadrant (e.g. Boddie and Cnaan 2006; Tirrito and Cascio 2003).

Any typology of faith-based welfare services will have its limitations (Dinham *et al.* 2009), not least of which includes considerable variation in praxis within and between religious traditions (Macey and Carling 2011). It is recognized that the predominant emphasis of organizations is not necessarily fixed within a particular quadrant and may vary both across time and between different programmes conducted by an agency. Furthermore, while recognizing that 'real organizations and programs rarely fit perfectly into ideal types' (Sider and Unruh 2004: 128), this framework demonstrates the diversity of faith-based welfare organizations, although it is recognized that the predominant quadrant(s) may vary in different religious and national contexts. Furthermore, although it has sometimes been proposed that the opposite of a programme or agency which is highly explicit in its religious identity is one with a secular orientation (e.g. Cnaan *et al.* 2003; Sider and Unruh 2004; Unruh and Sider 2005), the framework in Figure 1.1 recognizes that such distinctions have been questioned (e.g. Netting 2004; Whiting 2008; Dinham *et al.* 2009).

A further aspect of purpose relates to the financial aims of faith-based organizations. While faith-based welfare organizations tend to be non-profit voluntary organizations (Hiemstra 2002), they may need to generate some income to supplement state funding and donations. In some organizations this may lead to ensuring that the costs of providing the service are paid for by service users (Valins 2011). However, rather than requiring fees to be paid by the users of all services, the aims of some programmes may include generation of a profit which may be used to subsidize other services provided by the organization (Torry 2005).

Service provision

Often closely related to how an organization views its purpose is the nature of service provision. Faith-based welfare organizations range in scope from those offering a single service to large multi-programme and/or multi-site agencies which provide services to a wide range of needs within communities (Rogers *et al.* 2005) on a local, regional, national or international basis (Berger 2003). However, because of differing needs, resources and priorities in different communities, effective faith-based organizations need to find ways of working which are appropriate in and for the communities where they work (Barise 2005). In addition to being providers of welfare services, faith-based organizations may also be involved in public debates about the nature of service delivery (Angell 2010).

It is important to distinguish 'faith-placed' services which use the resources (e.g. buildings) of a religious group, but that are otherwise quite separate from 'faith-based' services which are provided by a religious organization either for its members or the wider community (Fagan *et al.* 2010). In delineating the place of professional social work from the broader activities of religious groups or organizations, Torry's definition of faith-based organizations is those 'organizations firmly related to a religious tradition but which do not have a religious activity as their primary aim' (2005: 3), and he argues that 'such organizations occupy a place between religious organizations and secular organizations, and deserve a treatment of their own' (2005: 3). This is in contrast with the more common binary view of organizations as either religious or secular (Linden 2008), although it is noted that in some countries, such as Greece (Fouka *et al.* 2012) and Italy (Bäckström *et al.* 2011), even the distinction between religious and secular is less than clear.

For Torry (2005), the difference between religious and faith-based organizations is not whether they are run by clergy or laity but rather the activities they undertake. Hence, as long as there is some religious connection or underpinning, the work cannot truly be called secular. Similarly, Belcher and DeForge (2007) have classified organizations on the basis of activities and, in their writing about social work in faith-based organizations, deliberately excluded services which sought to proselytize service users. Although no such exclusion was made in this current volume, the focus on faith-based organizations which employ professional social workers resulted in the majority of social workers interviewed working in organizations that would be categorized by Torry as 'faith based' rather than 'religious' and reflects that it is more common for social workers to be employed in community agencies than in local parishes where the primary aims are religious (Ebear *et al.* 2008).

For Unruh and Sider (2005), the critical question seems to be not whether the organization is faith based but whether or not the programmes it delivers are. They note that the programmes run by a single organization can range from those with a very explicit faith element in the programme, requiring staff to have a strong faith commitment consistent with the programme's emphasis, through to programmes with less explicit or no apparent faith content, and no religious requirements on the staff employed to run such programmes, with a range of types in between these ends of a continuum. As they consider a wide range of factors, including mission statement, founding, religious affiliation, organizational decision-making, sources of funding, in addition to religious content in programmes and staffing, Unruh and Sider demonstrate why there is such a broad range of organizations which come under the umbrella of being faith based. However, an important critique of their work is that Unruh and Sider have created a typology of faith-based organizations which best fits with direct practice and does not readily apply to other aspects of social work such as advocacy and policy development (Netting 2004).

Changing circumstances

Long-term survival has required many faith-based organizations to change, innovate and merge with other, similar organizations (Lake 2013). In doing so, the nature of religious expression can change significantly. Small local initiatives have sometimes given impetus to the emergence of large welfare agencies (e.g. Ferguson 2004; Holden and Trembath 2008) but while growth may result in faith-based organizations becoming economically more viable, it can also bring challenges for faith-based organizations in maintaining their faith identity. Similarly, as the needs of the target population change, faith-based organizations may need to redefine their purpose. In particular, it is has been recognized that as the needs of ethnic communities change, ethnic religious organizations providing welfare to their members sometimes find themselves with the potential capacity to provide services to members outside their communities (Boddie *et al.* 2011).

Changes sometimes result in organizations becoming independent of their founders. While Netting (1984) proposed that if an organizations calls itself faith based then it is, Torry (2005) has raised the question as to whether this can be so if the link with the founding vision or religious values is broken. This is particularly an issue concerning organizations which were originally established by religious groups and may have an ethos which reflects their religious origins but which are now community organizations with no formal links to religious groups (Middlemiss 2006b).

Conclusion

Faith-based organizations frequently claim themselves to be different from their secular counterparts whether this be in respect of what or how services are provided (Davies-Kildea 2007). Yet, despite such perceptions, as this chapter has demonstrated, there is no single definition as to what a faith-based organization is and against which claims of distinctiveness may be judged. Furthermore, Ebaugh *et al.* (2006) have previously concluded that there are multiple dimensions to religiosity among faith-based organizations and that scoring high on one of these dimensions is not a predictor of scoring highly on another. In particular, organizations which have a strong faith identity in terms of name or organizational structure often provide seemingly secular services where there is no explicit religious content (Vanderwoerd

2004). Thus, although this chapter has not been able to conclusively resolve the question of what is a faith-based organization, it does explain why seemingly very different organizations, in respect of their branding, organizational structure, purpose and service provision, can all claim to be faith based. And perhaps it is not how organizations perceive themselves but how they are perceived by others that is the critical question:

> What makes an organization 'faith-based?' ... It is not in these external variables of name or location or organizational type, then perhaps it is in the meaning given to the context by others. But who determines that meaning: the funders, administrators, service providers, recipients or some combination of these?
>
> (Rogers *et al.* 2005: 199)

The differing understandings of the various stakeholders in faith-based organizations will be further explored in Chapter 4. However, prior to this, Chapter 2 will consider the relationship of faith-based organizations with the welfare state, and in particular the impact of the state on faith-based organizations.

2

FAITH-BASED ORGANIZATIONS AND THE WELFARE STATE

> Religion has moved in public policy terms from being the Cinderella of the community and voluntary sector to being highly favoured, with millions of pounds of government money being pumped into helping faith groups become 'service provider' ready.
>
> (Baker 2012: 568)

Introduction

The term 'welfare state' has often been attributed to William Temple, who as Archbishop of Canterbury and head of the worldwide Anglican Union was seeking to make a distinction between Britain, and Germany which he regarded as a 'warfare state' (Ekstrand 2011; Lake 2013), although others have suggested that the notion of a welfare state first emerged in the late nineteenth century (Manow and van Kersbergen 2009). Although precise understandings as to what this involves have varied, in contemporary usage the term 'welfare state' generally refers to the social and economic contexts which support the well-being of the community and its members. While this includes welfare services provided directly to individuals and families, it also includes many other services provided (or funded) by the state which support the well-being of the community, for instance, social security payments and the public provision of services in areas such as health, housing and education. Economic policies which are associated with well-being both of individuals and the community, such as those concerned with taxation, superannuation and employment, may also be considered to be part of the concept of the welfare state (O'Connor et al. 2008).

In many countries, most welfare provision prior to the twentieth century was by religious organizations, but the state was not entirely disinterested in the welfare of individuals and communities. For example, in England the Poor Law Act of 1601, which was considered to be the most important policy development for dealing with poverty until the mid-nineteenth century, sought to distinguish between those who were poor and unable to support themselves such as the sick and elderly and whom the community ought to provide for, and those in reasonable health who had the capacity to obtain employment and in theory should have been able to support themselves (Alcock 1997). Whereas local parishes had responsibility for poor relief until the nineteenth century, increasing industrialization resulted in greater concentrations of the population living in cities and placed more pressure on local parishes in those areas for welfare provision than could be met by churches (Manow and van Kersbergen 2009).

As Baker (2012) reflects in the quote at the beginning of this chapter, the relationships between religious organizations and the state are not static, even where there have been long-term relationships (Leis-Peters 2010). During the twentieth century, the growing role of state provision of welfare and a lessened reliance on faith-based organizations occurred in many countries, and in some the role of faith-based welfare organizations continues to be in a state of flux, such as in Sweden where the disestablishment of the Church of Sweden in 2000 opened up new opportunities for the Church to play a role in the welfare state (Göcmen 2013).

In the UK, faith-based organizations were the providers of welfare services in the nineteenth century, supplanted by government after the Second World War. The role of the state was minimized in the 1980s, resulting in a mixed economy of welfare involving provision by both government and voluntary sector, with much more explicit involvement of the faith-based sector from 1997 (Dinham 2009), although as a Scottish social worker observed, the involvement of faith-based providers of social work services is often not acknowledged in Britain:

> I just think most of the social work it's that tradition across the board, adult, children and anything has come from faith roots. Mostly it was faith motivated people and organizations that started the basis of what has then become the welfare state and in a way, I think it's a shame that that isn't still at least recognized, that the contribution of people of faith have made to caring about each other, which has kind of changed into what I think has now become the welfare state, which to a great extent in the UK we can still be proud of, but I think has a lot of threats.

Within the UK, the range of services provided by faith-based organizations varies considerably between regions (Dinham 2009). Furthermore, the shape of the welfare state and the relative involvement of faith-based and other non-government providers of welfare services has not always emerged in a planned way and has sometimes been described as 'unsystematic, marginal and archaic' (Murphy 2006: 44.8), and may reflect the fact that within countries there is not necessarily a consensus as to whether there is a role for faith-based providers of welfare services, and if there is, what that role might be.

Welfare provision by the state often carries on religious traditions of providing for disadvantaged persons long established in a range of religions, including Christianity, Judaism and Islam (Cascio 2003). As one of the Scottish research participants responded in respect of a question about the relationship between faith-based organizations and the welfare state:

> I think it is quite easy to kind of pick up an argument that you have attempted the separation of church from state but I think there is quite a good role, actually. I think there is quite a positive role to see faith-based agencies playing a part in the delivery of social services and I suppose, historically, a lot of the social services were started and founded by various churches, so in that sense, I think there is a strength or a depth to the services there. I think in terms of religion, I think most religions would see the practice of the religion not simply in terms of going to church and participating in the services, but in living the faith in terms of charitable actions.

Despite the fact that it has sometimes been proposed that social welfare provision which is inspired by religious teaching is most likely to flourish in countries where Judaeo-Christian values predominate, social work may be found in countries with very different faith bases, including Islam, Buddhism and Hinduism (Cox 1995). In respect of Islam, the pillars of faith include a responsibility for community members to provide for the practical needs of those who were unable to provide for themselves. Expectations of the faithful, such as tithing, ensured a version of a welfare state going back centuries, although evidence of this may be difficult to find in some modern Islamic states, such that:

> Indeed, the Muslim in a Western setting might well believe that modern laws around the likes of welfare and non-discrimination, designed to protect and guarantee the rights of all with special emphasis on the poor and disadvantaged, were initially inspired by Islam.
>
> (Lovat 2010: 190)

Welfare states

The relationship between religious welfare organizations and the state may vary considerably between countries, including the size and scope of the state's involvement in welfare (Castles 2002) and the level of political debate about this involvement (Larson and Robertson 2007). Yet unless individuals have worked or lived in other countries, they may take it for granted that the status quo in their own country in respect of the role of faith-based organizations in welfare provision is the only way possible (Bäckström and Davie 2010) and fail to recognize that the form of welfare state which has been adopted by a country can reflect the political climate (Prochaska 2006), as well as the dominant religious traditions present (Yeung *et al.* 2006). In Europe, the mainly Protestant North has welfare provision largely coordinated by the state or local authorities, whereas in the more Catholic South the tendency is for welfare services to be provided by religious orders or confraternities (Jawad 2012a). There may also be differences in how faith-based organizations should be organized. For example, in Nordic countries there is an expectation that this occurs at the local (i.e. parish) level, whereas in Italy there is the expectation that this is provided by religious organizations or religious orders serving larger regions (Pettersson 2011).

Esping-Andersen's (1990) identification of three distinct models of welfare states provides a useful starting point for considering the impact of different religious traditions on welfare states. In the Social Democratic model, which typifies welfare provision in Scandinavian countries, the state has responsibility for the provision of core services, with voluntary organizations, including churches, providing additional or complementary services to those provided by the state. In the Liberal model, often associated with Anglophone countries such as the UK, US, Australia, Canada and New Zealand, the state has primary responsibility for ensuring that key services are provided but may do so in conjunction with non-government agencies, whereas the Conservative model, present in many continental European nations, has a more limited role for the state in direct welfare provision and a corresponding emphasis on provision by other service providers, including faith-based organizations, where possible. Although the detail of Esping-Anderson's model has been widely critiqued both within and beyond Europe (Jawad 2009; Kahl 2005), there is nevertheless some credibility in the proposition that the scope of services provided by faith-based organizations is likely to vary depending on the model of welfare state (Bäckström and Davie 2010), as are the expectations of members of the community in respect of service provision by faith-based organizations (Pettersson 2011).

One factor which Esping-Anderson's model does not take into account but which is also critical in understanding the role of faith-based welfare organizations is the relationship between the state and the dominant religion (Manow and van Kersbergen 2009). In countries where there is a state religion, there may be little or no separation between the religious institutions and the state. Several European countries have state churches where technically the Church is part of the state and under state rule. Hence, in Greece it has been suggested that there is welfare service which is church- and state-run, with a third group of private organizations with links to the church or religion (Fokas 2006). Similarly, issues emerge in the Middle East where Islamic organizations are among the largest and most effective welfare organizations (Clark 2008). Identifying whether organizations are state run or faith based in Saudi Arabia where the monarchy is closely tied to Islam is far from straightforward (Kroessin and Mohamed 2008), as it is in other countries where Islam has been adopted as the state religion such as Iran where religious welfare is a para-state activity with a strong emphasis on social control (Saedi 2004).

The role of faith-based organizations versus the welfare state

Having considered the differing potential for the involvement of faith-based organizations in various models of welfare states, this chapter will now turn to exploring arguments for faith-based organizations playing at most a minimal role in the welfare state, as well as arguments for faith-based organizations having a legitimate role in the provision of non-core welfare services, and working in collaboration with the state in the provision of essential welfare services. Finally, this chapter will consider the suggestion that an important role for faith-based organizations is to act as a community watchdog and advocate for members of the community whose welfare needs are considered not to be well served by the welfare state. These roles are not necessarily mutually incompatible.

Limited or no role for faith-based organizations

The very potential, if not existence, of faith-based welfare brings out opponents arguing that it should not exist (Gilligan 2010) and in some instances explicit attempts to remove welfare provision from religious organizations. For example, during the 1960s in the newly independent Tanzania, the government was determined to nationalize welfare services as part of efforts to gain power over the churches which until then had been the main providers of welfare services within the country. However, the Tanzanian government failed to achieve its objective due to the ability of the faith-based organizations to attract much-needed funds from foreign donors which would not necessarily have contributed to the costs of running welfare services under the aegis of the Tanzanian government (Jennings 2008).

A more widespread objection to the existence of faith-based organizations involves concerns as to their ability to provide a professional service which best serves the needs of community members (DeHart 2010). Although Ashford and Timms' (1990) study of English social workers revealed no difference between the practice standards of social workers in faith-based organizations compared to their colleagues in statutory agencies, in Germany it has been claimed that the professionalization of social work is a direct consequence of the secularization of social welfare during the twentieth century (Brauns and Kramer 1995). Fearing that this would be a regressive step for social work practice, in some countries, including Italy, social workers have been critical of the idea of placing social work under the authority of the church. In particular, they fear the church will simply try to fill the gaps of the state welfare system and perpetuate systems which have exploited women as caregivers (Frisina 2006). Such arguments represent a fundamental belief that religion and the state are so intrinsically different that it is not possible for both to be involved in welfare provision. Furthermore, it has been argued that expecting such differing institutions to collaborate in providing for the welfare of the population potentially damages both the state and the religious organizations it seeks to work with:

> We can readily agree on two things. First, religion and state represent different human institutions. One is primarily concerned with the other-worldly destiny of the human soul, the other with the affairs of this world. One is a matter of belief and cannot be coerced, the other deals with matters requiring conformity and had coercion built into its structure. One talks in terms of largely non-negotiable absolutes, the other aims at a carefully assembled and inherently tentative consensus. Since the two are so different in their orientation, a close alliance between them is the surest way to corrupt and undermine both.
>
> (Parekh 2009: v)

The desire to ensure that the state and religion are kept separate can result in a failure by state authorities to recognize and use the contributions which faith-based organizations can make to the wider community (Cnaan and Newman 2010). The legitimacy of the state compared to other service providers may be enhanced if social work is reserved to refer only to services provided by the state. Social services provided by the Lutheran church in Finland are referred to as 'diaconia' rather than social work which refers to services provided by local municipalities. Despite having common roots, ethical bases and ways of working, as diaconia services are not paid for by the state, they are not necessarily recognized as being social work (Jokela 2011).

It has sometimes been observed that the welfare state may be characterized as a secularized version of the Church's commitment to providing charity (Taylor 1995). This is particularly the case in Scandanavia, Germany and England, where strong welfare states emerged during the twentieth century. The state churches saw no reason to establish separate welfare services of their own (Fix and Fix 2002; Manow and van Kersbergen 2009), and there were many instances where they withdrew from forms of service delivery which had been taken over by the secular welfare state (Jawad 2012a).

CASE STUDY: THE CHURCH OF ENGLAND AFTER THE SECOND WORLD WAR

From the late nineteenth century, there were a growing number of people within England's churches who believed that their organizations no longer had the capacity to provide for the health and welfare needs of the nation's poor. Research evidence collected in the latter years of the nineteenth and early years of the twentieth century by William Booth who founded the Salvation Army, and philanthropists Seebohm Rowntree and Charles Booth all declared that more than a quarter of the English population was living in dire poverty. Church leaders, aware that the efforts of individual parishes would be piecemeal and insufficient, began arguing for a welfare state. Old age pensions were introduced in 1908 and a compulsory national insurance scheme, which would provide for individuals in certain circumstances if they became ill or unemployed, commenced in 1911 (Prochaska 2006).

Faith-based welfare has played in important role in nation building in countries such as Britain (Jawad 2012b). As did other sectors of British society, churches contributed to the nation's war efforts in the First and Second World Wars, providing support to both those who had gone abroad to fight, and also caring for those who remained within the country. After 1938, many women who had until then undertaken charitable work through their local parishes joined the Women's Voluntary Service (WVS), doing charitable work as required by the state. Not only did the war effort take away volunteers from the churches, but the number of clergy dropped significantly. Prior to the First World War, there had been 20,000 Anglican clergy in England and Wales, but by 1950 this had decreased to around 15,000. The churches of Britain also suffered major losses of buildings as a result of bombing raids, with approximately 15,000 experiencing damage, many of which were destroyed (Prochaska 2006).

Such was the impact of the Second World War on both the churches, and on British society more generally, that the previous welfare regimes which had assumed a significant role for the churches was no longer a viable proposition. With the introduction of both the National Assistance Act providing a universal social security scheme and the establishment of the National Health Service providing universal health care, 1948 marks the beginning of the modern welfare state in Britain (Prochaska 2006):

> This was a period of high idealism whose effect, despite all good intentions, was to recast the widespread, experienced and highly effective network of non-government providers, many of which were faith-based, as outside the strategic idealism of government. The needs of post-war Britain were seen as too important to be left to the well-meaning amateurs. This also had an instant effect on their funding since the welfare state encouraged the expectation that needs would be met without resort to charity, and giving and philanthropy suffered accordingly.
>
> (Dinham 2009: 123)

Deliberations by the Church of England bishops in 1948 declared the welfare state to embody Christian morality (Prochaska 2006) and that it was no longer the role of the Church to be the mainstay of welfare provision (Jawad 2012a). In subsequent decades, it became apparent that the state could not provide for every welfare need of community members, and the need for additional services provided by churches and other local organizations was recognized (Prochaska 2006). To some extent, the myth of the welfare state remains pervasive and the participation of religious groups in welfare provision has often lacked public acknowledgement (Harris *et al.* 2003). Whiting (2008) has argued that the at most ad hoc and piecemeal approach of the Church of England to involvement in welfare provision distinguished it from the other major churches both in and beyond Britain which had continued their involvements in welfare provision.

In recent years, the Church of England has moved on from its post-war stance and has been actively considering how it can play a role in welfare provision in England in the twenty-first century, not only examining its own capacity but exploring how the Anglican Church plays a role in welfare provision in other countries (Davis *et al.* 2008). It is perhaps unlikely that in the near future the Church of England will return to being a prominent provider of welfare services in England, but greater recognition within and outside the Church that it can work in conjunction with the state and contribute to the well-being of the English people is not an unrealistic proposition. On the other side of the equation will be the question as to on what basis the state may be prepared to work in partnership with the Church of England and whether that will be acceptable to the Church. Dinham and Lowndes (2008: 831) quote a Church of England activist who commented that 'the government doesn't want to hear about what makes us faithful people. They'll fund us if we don't do anything religious with the money.'

Faith-based organizations as providers of residual services

Where the emergence of strong welfare states in the mid-twentieth century resulted in faith-based organizations no longer playing a major role in welfare provision in fields where the state assumed responsibility, religious groups were often forced to reconsider their role in society. Yet many recognized that welfare provision was what they did because it fitted in with their values and beliefs. As one Australian social worker reflected:

> The provision of welfare obviously sits well with their values, and they're not about profit, and they're not even so much about glory, so in some ways welfare is hard and in a time when it's all about economic rationalism and doing more with less, and efficiencies and all of that, which just make it harder, I think that they add value.

Rather than cease involvement in welfare provision, some faith-based organizations moved the focus of their work to activities which supplemented state provision, providing services to those for whom state provision has been insufficient. For example, the Church of Finland considers its role to provide services to those most in need and not otherwise provided with services (Jokela 2011). As an Australian research participant remarked: 'We still do a lot of emergency food relief, financial assistance and all that sort of thing.' Another made the point:

> I think the Church, to their credit and most of the Christian churches, if you look at most of the big care organizations around, and welfare organizations around Victoria and Australia they have been started by churches, and I think they've grown up out of people who have had that concept and that vision of, God wants to sit with the poor and if he wants to sit with people who are hurting. . . .

Others have sought to complement state provision (Schwartz *et al.* 2008), particularly in areas in which they have expertise. Hence, in Sweden it has been suggested that the role of the Church in welfare provision is most appropriate when the Church is providing services using its expertise, such as in counselling (Edgardh Beckman *et al.* 2006) and in the UK faith-based organizations are significant providers of services in the fields of homelessness and adoption (Furness and Gilligan 2012). Conversely, in Australia it has been proposed that the state has often recognized the expertise of faith-based organizations and sought to partner with them to extend the range of services available in the community (Quinlan 2008). While sometimes this was in response to particular short-term needs (Lake 2013), at other times this has been for ongoing needs, and in the past has included care of the elderly, marriage counselling and residential care of children. Through funding agreements, governments gained greater capacity to set expectations in respect of standards of care and professional qualifications held by staff (Swain 2009).

Despite faith-based organizations often being at the vanguard of providing services for those who are socially excluded (Angell 2010), religious communities don't necessarily always have the capacity to provide welfare services to their own communities (Paton *et al.* 2009), let alone to other communities in areas most in need (Quinlan 2008). Furthermore, governments should not assume that faith-based organizations will be present to partner with them in service provision in some communities (Larson and Robertson 2007). Moreover, faith-based organizations may be quite selective as to whom they are willing to provide services. In Australia, while religious groups have provided welfare for a wide range of groups including children, single mothers, people living with a disability and the elderly, some sectors of the population such as those with mental illness and prisoners were a less attractive option for many faith-based organizations and care of these groups has remained predominantly the responsibility of the state (Swain 2009).

Faith-based organizations in many countries have developed reputations for establishing innovative services which governments have not set up or seen the need for (Holden and Trembath 2008; Scales 2011). This is in respect of both newly emerging social issues (Fix and Fix 2002) and where the design of existing services is unable to address the needs of service users (Gardner 2006). As an Australian social worker explained, 'I think because we align our self with the gospel, we are called or compelled in a way, in a way to be responsive but to also to be innovative . . . to be open to possibility.' Whereas state-provided services are often highly bureaucratic and rule bound, there may be more scope for flexibility in approach by faith-based organizations (Edgardh Beckman *et al.* 2006). As an Australian social worker working in a small community-based service reflected:

> It doesn't have to be church-run, but the churches are the obvious sort of mobs to do it, I think, because they've got the kind of mind-set for this kind of stuff, and the heart for it. I think, but it doesn't have to be run through a church, but these kind of community sort of models, to be alive in different suburbs around the place, because really, we cater for a lot of people where we're only in one little part of [City].

Faith-based organizations which have strong community links have often been able to reach parts of the population which may not be reached by other service providers (Fagan *et al.* 2010; Paton *et al.* 2009), particularly those whose experiences of social exclusion are reinforced by public policy initiatives (Edwards 2013). As another Australian research participant commented:

> You know what we hope to do and we want to try and hold onto is that closeness to our community and that social capital that we all know that is sort of the gold nugget in terms of community development. So the relationships, that's really, really important to us and I think we have that.

It is often noted that faith-based organizations go beyond recognizing the most pressing welfare needs and, where possible, seek to meet their spiritual needs. This doesn't necessarily mean any overt discussion of religious beliefs or practices, but may simply reflect an orientation which regards a person as being much more than their material and physical needs (Fokas 2006). As a Jewish social worker has observed about Catholic hospices:

> [A] lot of the hospices are affiliated to religions, particularly Catholics. I once had a problem with that, you walk in and it's blue carpet with

soft music and crosses everywhere, but then I guess that's where they have found there was a need and they've funded the care, whereas it wasn't done in the mainstream. There isn't enough mainstream care for people that offers a spiritual side but is not affiliated to a structured religion.

('Kate' in Gardner 2011: 153)

CASE STUDY: FAITH-BASED SOCIAL WORK IN SCOTLAND

Since the creation of the welfare state in Scotland in the late 1940s, it has been accepted that there is a need for services in addition to what the state can offer (Bondi 2011). The Church of Scotland's welfare organization, Crossreach, is currently one of the largest non-government welfare organizations in Scotland, employing approximately 2,000 staff (Crossreach 2013a), some of whom hold a professional social work qualification (Church of Scotland 2013). Like many non-government providers in the social care sector, Crossreach is a member of the Coalition of Care and Support Providers in Scotland (CCSPS), which collectively employ 45,000 staff (Coalition of Care and Support Providers in Scotland 2013) as well as many other voluntary sector welfare initiatives that are not members of CCSPS, some of which are faith-based:

> In reality, the Christian churches in Scotland continue to carry out a wide range of social work activity. Much social work practice in the voluntary sector in Scotland remains funded by Christian churches and organisations, even when these agencies choose to play down their Christian connections. It is the Church of Scotland, the Roman Catholic Church, the Scottish Episcopal Church and the Salvation Army which carries out most of the work with destitute and homeless people in Scotland today, as well as substantial provision for older people and projects which work with 'outcast' groups such as prostitutes, drug users and people with alcohol problems.
>
> (Cree 1996: 25)

On this basis, seeking to interview social workers employed in faith-based organizations in Scotland seemed a reasonable proposition, but in practice proved much more difficult. In the five interviews conducted with Scottish social workers, the question as to why it had been difficult to locate social workers in Scottish faith-based organizations was explored, and this shed light on the relationship between faith-based organizations and the welfare state in Scotland.

One suggestion why social workers are not found in large numbers in faith-based organizations is cost. As one participant remarked: 'Well you could be cynical and say, it's just it's more expensive to employ social workers.' But even when they did employ social workers, in some organizations participants noted that their salaries were much lower than had they been employed in statutory settings and

unlikely to attract social workers who did not have a strong personal commitment to working there. Funding for faith-based organizations is often
limited and insufficient. A Scottish social worker in a different organization
commented:

> However we are very strapped for cash and the big frustration is every three
> years you go into a bidding kind of thing for money, you know, with certain
> funding agencies that we go with and you approach that time with a bit of
> fear, tension and pressure and staff are getting itchy about their jobs and
> that.

However, in this respect Scottish faith-based organizations are no different from
other voluntary sector welfare organizations in Scotland. As another Scottish
participant noted:

> Well I think in the UK the government is pulling a lot of funding from social
> care organizations and over the last five or six years, quite a number of
> organizations have been shut down or have had to reform and re-resurrect
> themselves in a different format, so there's less government money for
> organizations that help vulnerable people. So, I think the Christian organiza-
> tions are in an important place, in terms of really getting the Christian
> community behind them to provide financial and practical support to really,
> I guess, back up what the government's doing or even take the lead.

In response to such concerns, the Church of Scotland at the 2013 General Assembly
noted that it was not in a position to step in and further subsidize the costs of
programmes it was delivering on behalf of local authorities and other statutory
organizations:

> We are very much aware of the funding constraints placed upon Local
> Authorities and statutory funders and are committed, as far as possible, to
> work with them to achieve the best possible outcomes for people who use
> our services. Indeed we have over recent years achieved major cost
> efficiencies to ensure that we are providing best value. However, in order to
> maintain the quality of our services we cannot meet additional cost pressures
> from our existing resources nor accept funding cuts. This will be an ongoing
> challenge over the coming year and we will have to seriously consider the
> viability of services if funders seek cost savings or the provision of additional
> services within existing funding.
>
> (Church of Scotland 2013: 6/15)

A second reason for not employing social workers is that faith-based organizations
may be unaware of the skill-set which social workers bring to their work and
why there may be good reasons to employ a social worker even if not required

to do so. Reflecting on the faith-based sector in Scotland more generally, the manager of one organization which is committed to employing qualified social workers said:

> I think that there's almost a sense within the church that these kind of things shouldn't be overly professionalized. That actually they should be sort of ordinary people responding to the needs of the vulnerable as a kind of faith mission, not necessarily as a professional sort of motivation. I'm only saying that that's my opinion. I don't know, but we wonder about that.

Another noted that without social workers, social perspectives may have little influence in programme planning and delivery:

> I was quite struck by . . . there weren't many social workers employed at the [faith-based organization] and you would get a lot of nursing staff employed there. I think that is an indication for the kind of ethos and role that the agency can provide. For example . . . a lot of the services at one point were residential based, so you would bring that health model into that and I think the social model about community development wasn't really developed.

In some organizations a seeming absence of social workers may reflect the position titles used rather than there being no qualified social workers on the staff. Within Scottish society, including the social work community, there is a tendency to consider 'social work' to be a profession based within the bureaucracy (Cree 1996) undertaking particular forms of social intervention on the basis of a legal mandate with only limited scope for the profession in the non-government sector (Jawad 2012b). A not uncommon perspective of Scottish social workers as articulated by one research participant is as follows:

> I mean I see the social work role always anyway being broadened than just what you do in children and families nowadays and it is that bit about engaging with people, showing empathy, helping them by empowering them and helping them to move on and make changes in their lives. And I suppose the difference here is that we're not so much agents of the law although we work with the law. Do you know what I mean? We are not charged with having to be supervisory social workers from a Children's Hearing or something like that where it would be an involving the permanency process or anything but we contribute to that.

The effect of positioning social work as essentially being confined to statutory work results in a congruence between the work of social workers and the essential roles of the welfare state. Within such thinking, it becomes difficult to consider faith-based organizations in Scotland as having any role in relation to the welfare state other than as a provider of residual services. Hence, for faith-based organizations to play a greater role in respect of the welfare state, a change of thinking about the nature of social work would need to occur. As a social worker in a different organization reflected:

> I suppose the difficulty is that social work tends to be given regularly to them in the sense that, at the moment, statutory work can't be given out to voluntary organizations but that may well come as this government starts to develop in outsourcing the work. But yes, I think because a lot of social workers had done statutory work, you know, children on formal supervision orders and the like and probation orders, at the moment, that can only be done by the authority, so I think that's why that is.

Faith-based organizations as providers of essential services

In many countries there is a prevailing view that it is the role of the state to provide key services which other organizations cannot, or there is a belief that they should not, be providing (Jawad 2009). However, there is frequently a lack of consensus within countries as to which services should be run by the state and which should be run by faith-based or other non-government organizations, and it may be that supply rather than demand for faith-based services results in religion being a key force in welfare provision (Jawad 2009). For example, in Australia during the twentieth century, the reliance on churches to run services varied considerably between states, with the Tasmanian government taking full responsibility for orphanages and children's homes when such services were mostly provided by faith-based organizations in other states. Similar variations occurred in Canadian provinces (Murphy 2006).

In many countries, the state actually relies on faith-based organizations to deliver a wide range of social services and has long provided funds to faith-based organizations to enable them to carry out this role (Schwartz *et al.* 2008). For example, in Germany, agencies associated with Catholic and Protestant churches constitute the largest two providers of welfare services, albeit funded by the state and delegated by the state to provide services (Pettersson 2011). As an Australian social worker noted, faith-based organizations have frequently demonstrated a capacity to deliver services on behalf of the state:

> I don't see any tensions in it, I just see people out there that need some help, I don't see any conflict of interest there between us. I think we're doing a very good job of what the state needs to be done, caring for people often in really difficult circumstances some of their troubles are just enormous we help all kinds. I think we're just doing the work that the state needs to have done.

But acting as an agent of the state is not necessarily unproblematic, especially when:

> There is no clear dividing line between public and voluntary social services. The intermingling of funds, the blurring of roles, and the resulting issues surrounding autonomy and accountability are well documented. Church-related agencies, being a subcategory of the voluntary sector, are no exception.
>
> (Netting 1982: 586)

Hence, as one Australian research participant replied when asked about the role of faith-based organizations in respect of the welfare state:

> To answer your question, within faith-based organizations, I think there is a perspective of faith-based organizations being part of the welfare state. . . . So in the welfare sector, do they have a role? I think so, but I believe they need to be very well structured.

In many countries, faith-based organizations need to compete with other organizations for public tenders (Leis-Peters 2010) but small organizations may not have the capacity to meet the financial and other reporting require-ments associated with such funding arrangements (Dinham 2009; Yancey *et al.* 2004). In the state of Victoria in Australia where most of the research interviews were undertaken, over the past two decades the state government, which funds most welfare programmes in Victoria, has moved away from grant funding to approved organizations and in many programme areas now requires potential service providers to compete in tender processes (Swain 2009). Many small faith-based organizations merged to form large conglomerates in the 1990s which had the infrastructure to engage with the state on this basis. However, this can place faith-based organizations at risk of taking on what may be regarded as the more undesirable characteristics of the state (DiMaggio and Powell 1983) in terms of becoming bureauc-ratic and impersonal. As the manager of a large Victorian faith-based organization reflected:

> I think that one of the very awkward things that is happening in this sector at this point is, to survive you have to become big and to provide the service you have to become big to then have the required infra-structure that you need to be accountable and all sorts of other things. At the same time, in becoming big I think there is a real risk of losing the relational component that a lot of faith-based agencies would have operated on, because while they are not coming in from a corporate world they are being forced into becoming, forced in lots of ways, depending on how it's done, to becoming much more appropriately professional.

While the desire of states to have faith-based and other non-government organizations deliver services on their behalf can be underpinned by a strong rationale such as faith-based organizations being closer to the communities they serve (Leis-Peters 2010), the motivations for the state to enter such collaborations are not always noble. Faith-based organizations may be regarded favourably if they are perceived to have lower running costs than other organizations, particularly if they are able to harness resources, including volunteer or inexpensive labour. They often also have additional resources which they provide (Orji 2011). As the former manager of a faith-based organization with an annual budget of several million Australian dollars reflected about the role of faith-based organizations in relation to the state:

> I certainly think there's a role. The role might be for the wrong reason. . . . There's never enough resources to provide the service that's required. So, for instance, I know the [Organization] put a lot of their own fundraising money into the work, their social work, which – so the government receives . . . certainly over half a million bucks. . . . So that's value-added for the government.

It is not just in Australia where government programmes are substantially subsidized by faith-based organizations. Jason Davies-Kildea (2007), an Australian Salvation Army officer, discovered this to be a common feature of faith-based organizations he visited as part of a study tour to the US, UK and Kenya. The possibility of organizations being able and willing to subsidize welfare provision on top of what they receive from the state is an attractive option for governments in an era of fiscal constraints. For example, during the 1980s, President Reagan urged US faith-based organizations to help compensate for cutbacks in federal funding of welfare programmes (Yancey *et al.* 2009). More recently, such cost-cutting strategies have been advanced through the promotion of welfare pluralism in which the state and other organizations collaborate to deliver services as part of New Public Management strategies in a number of countries (Angell and Wyller 2006; Conradson 2011). Even if not necessarily apparent at the outset, the long-term agenda of the state may be to withdraw from service delivery as far as possible, reflecting a shift from rights-based welfare provision to that of addressing only the most pressing needs (Challen 1996). In doing so, the state may have no qualms about exploiting the goodwill of faith-based and other charitable organizations by failing to adequately resource them to work on its behalf (Gilligan 2010). Ultimately, this may be to the detriment of faith-based organizations and to those who are in receipt of services:

> Faith communities with a long tradition of volunteering and philanthropy are particularly vulnerable to being co-opted by the state

> into doing something for nothing. This is neither just nor in the long-term likely to produce sustainable high quality community services, and therefore should be resisted by religious groups when they enter into partnerships or contracts with the authorities.
>
> (Smith 2002: 174)

Faith groups are active providers in areas of social care at the edges of society where other providers have often withdrawn services (Dinham 2012a), and during a period of state cutbacks three of the four largest faith-based organizations in Christchurch, New Zealand were ensuring that community needs were met by subsidizing the costs of service delivery from their financial reserves (Conradson 2011). In the longer term, such strategies are likely to be unviable and hence there are growing suggestions that perhaps faith-based organizations need to reconsider their role in respect of the state and refuse to be complicit with expectations that they will subsidize the work of the state:

> A major question for the majority churches, for example, is how to react to cutbacks in welfare provision. Should the churches adopt a critical role in relation to the reduced ambitions of the state, or should churches enter the stakes themselves as welfare entrepreneurs, taking over areas of service abandoned by the state?
>
> (Pettersson 2011: 16)

In Finland, it has been suggested that the state, by referring services users to the churches for financial support, was then able to justify cuts in the state welfare budget (Jokela 2011). Finland is not the only country to have adopted such logic. Neoliberal reforms in the 1990s in New Zealand resulted in faith-based organizations stepping in to provide services once provided by the state to the poorest members of the community, including the unemployed, homeless and elderly (Conradson 2011). In Australia over the past two decades there have been a number of incidents when conservative governments have sought to reduce expenditure on social welfare by suggesting that services should be provided by the non-government sector more generally, but particularly those associated with the various religions (Lake 2013). At times this has resulted in government announcements that the delivery of particular services would be devolved to high-profile faith-based organizations, without any consultation of those organizations (Holden and Trembath 2008). Some programmes which governments have sought to devolve have been regarded by many faith-based organizations as morally repugnant and they have chosen not to become involved in these programmes. This includes programmes for the unemployed in which the faith-based organizations would have been required to be punitive towards job-seekers who had not been able to comply with conditions associated with their social security payments in situations when a more compassionate response would have been warranted (Davis *et al.* 2008).

There may nevertheless be benefits to faith-based organizations from collaborating with the welfare state, even if this has come about due to budget issues (DeHart 2010), although as the following case example demonstrates, this is not necessarily straightforward and should not be assumed.

CASE STUDY: 'CHARITABLE CHOICE' FUNDING IN THE US

There has been much public interest and debate in the US on the role of faith-based organizations since the mid-1990s with the introduction of the Personal Responsibility and Work Opportunity Reconciliation Act 1996, which included a section about the role of faith-based organizations and has become known as 'Charitable Choice' (Cnaan and Boddie 2002). This provided new, but not uncontroversial, opportunities for faith-based agencies to receive state funding. Prior to this initiative, a strict separation between the state and religion resulted in state funding only being available to faith-based organizations for programmes which were entirely secular at the point of service delivery, but the changes resulted in a relaxation of this requirement, enabling faith-based organizations and programmes to apply for federal and state funding which they had previously not been eligible to apply for (Bacon 2011; Smith and Teasley 2009). For instance, although no funds were to be spent on religious worship or other religious activities, including activities essentially concerned with religious conversion, 'Charitable Choice' enshrined the rights of religious organizations to determine their religious character and expression of religious beliefs, including displays of religious symbols as well as inviting service users to participate in activities which were ostensibly of a religious nature. Furthermore, having a faith basis could not of itself be grounds for organizations receiving state funding (Bacon 2011). However, at the same time, the legislation required that the religious freedom of service users be maintained. In other words, potential service users could not be discriminated against on the basis of their religious beliefs and, if service users objected to the religious character of an organization, the state had an obligation to ensure that alternate service providers were available (Davis 1996).

The 'Charitable Choice' provision was part of widespread welfare reforms in the US commencing in the mid-1990s (Austin 2003). It reflected the view of some sectors of the community which believed that faith-based and other voluntary organizations should take more responsibility for caring for disadvantaged members of the community and not leave this to the state (Cnaan *et al.* 1999) and were willing to do so (Pipes and Ebaugh 2002). At the same there were concerns about the effectiveness of many programmes provided by the state to alleviate poverty (Williamson and Hodges 2006) and often untested claims that the faith-based sector could deliver services more efficiently and effectively (Cnaan and

Boddie 2006; Wuthnow *et al.* 2004) or that programmes staffed by people of faith would be more effective (Unruh and Sider 2005). With limited evidence to substantiate or refute claims about the ability of faith-based organizations to deliver the desired outcomes or evidence that any efficacy was actually faith-related (Ferguson *et al.* 2007), some have claimed that the 'overly simplistic' (Smith and Sosin 2001: 652) thinking underpinning the move to 'Charitable Choice' essentially reflected an ideological shift in US policy-making (Farnsley 2001). A more cynical view is that 'Charitable Choice' enabled the state to spend less on welfare provision by taking advantage of the eagerness of some faith-based organizations to receive state funding without having a well-formed understanding of the true costs associated with delivering on these contracts (Austin 2003; Bacon 2011). Furthermore,

> Cutting programs that force people to seek help from religious organizations is not the optimum way to create the type of local system that is everyone's ideal: a system that is humane, caring, responsive and cost-effective.
>
> (Cnaan *et al.* 1999: 20)

Faith-based organizations funded under the 'Charitable Choice' provision were nevertheless subject to the same accounting and reporting regimes as were other funded organizations (Davis 1996). In particular, faith-based organizations needed to be able to demonstrate that the services they were providing were at least as effective, and preferably more effective, than services being provided by other welfare organizations. This was far from straightforward, as existing evaluation methodologies then in use in US welfare organizations made little or no reference to religious beliefs or practices. Moreover, given the diversity of religious belief and expression, the need for a more nuanced understanding of social work practice in faith-based organizations emerged (Boddie and Cnaan 2006). Hence, researchers such as Cnaan *et al.* (2003) and Sider and Unruh (2004) undertook work which focused on explicit expressions of religion in the management and staffing of organizations, the extent to which religious content service users are exposed through their interactions in the agency and/or with agency staff, and the extent of expectations that service users would participate in religious activities, have religious experiences or undergo religious conversion.

The ability of faith-based organizations to deliver contracted services has been variable. On balance, while supporters often claim they are more effective than other agencies delivering similar services, the evidence would tend to suggest they don't provide an inferior service to that provided by non-faith-based organizations (Cnaan and Newman 2010). However, effective service delivery requires more than a well-designed programme, and faith-based organizations which have insufficiently developed administrative infrastructures, including mechanisms for staff recruitment and management, may struggle to deliver what is required (DeHart 2010).

Faith-based organizations as watchdog

Although open to debate, one role of religious groups is to participate in public debate about welfare issues (Davis *et al.* 2008; Middlemiss 2006b). Hence, irrespective of the scope and extent to which faith-based organizations provide services to individuals and communities, religious groups are often found to be prominent voices in the community, advocating for the needs of those who are excluded, including the poor (Ebear *et al.* 2008; Swain 2009), the homeless (Conradson 2011), and refugees and asylum seekers (Cemlyn and Briskman 2003), as well as acting as a community watchdog in respect of service provision by the state (Chapman 2009):

> Deregulation swept away the fixtures of economic life, smaller government removed the mechanisms of public support, the maxim of user pays eroded the ethos of the fair go. The churches emerged in the late twentieth century to care for many of the casualties the state had abandoned, and to help articulate the residue social conscience.
>
> (Macintyre 1999: 265)

Working in solidarity with vulnerable and marginalized groups often opens religious organizations to criticism and attempts to silence them. In extreme situations, religious groups which have offered sanctuary to refugees and displaced persons have become subject to violent attacks (Parsitau 2011). In the case of faith-based welfare organizations which receive state funding, the silencing tends to be more subtle, playing on the fear of organizations losing their funding (Glennon 2000). In Australia, it is not uncommon for funding agreements between government and non-government organizations, including faith-based organizations, to include restrictions on the funded organization being able to speak out against government policy in areas associated with their funding. In countries where there is a state church or religion to which the majority of the population are affiliated, the question has been asked if it is realistic to expect faith-based organizations to be critical of the state (Edgardh and Pettersson 2010). Hence,

> In countries where the welfare involvement of the churches and the church-related organizations is extensive and institutionalized, their position *vis-à-vis* public debate is complex. On the one hand, the churches are fully accepted as professional actors in the field of welfare. On the other, the fact that they are so closely related to the state means that it is difficult for them to criticize the system of which they are part.
>
> (Pettersson 2011: 42)

Consistent with this is the observation that in the Finnish context, social welfare staff employed by the state church provide services but do not speak out against or show any inclination to influence social policy (Jokela 2011). Nevertheless, even organizations which receive funding from or work in close cooperation with the state can maintain a strong advocacy role (Ebaugh *et al.* 2005). As to how faith-based organizations can be involved in both service delivery and play a leading role in welfare reform is demonstrated in the following case study of the Brotherhood of St Laurence, in Melbourne, Australia.

CASE STUDY: THE BROTHERHOOD OF ST LAURENCE

Founded as a religious order of the Anglican Church in 1930, the Brotherhood of St Laurence moved to Fitzroy, a then impoverished inner city suburb of Melbourne in 1933 to work with the poor. Although the religious order did not survive, what emerged was a social welfare agency which throughout its history has pioneered new responses to address poverty. From early on, the Brotherhood has sought not just to provide material relief to those experiencing poverty, but also to address the fundamental causes and effects of poverty and inequalities. Campaigning for justice and social reform very quickly became part of the Brotherhood's mission, and continues to this day alongside its activities in service provision to those experiencing the effects of poverty and disadvantage (BSL 2013). In 2012 the 'Guiding principles' identified by the Brotherhood included 'To be a national voice on poverty and exclusion' and 'To develop innovative policy, programs and practice' (BSL 2012: 1).

The Brotherhood has been involved in public policy for almost all of its history, and this is firmly ingrained in the culture of the organization. Its first forays into public policy development emerged in the 1940s as a response to the poor-quality housing, regarded as the 'worst slum in Melbourne', in the streets around their headquarters. Films of the living conditions were made, and staff members of the Brotherhood were involved in protests against unfair laws for tenants and landlords. The clearance of the slums and the establishment of Victoria's public housing authority came about in part as a response to efforts by the Brotherhood of St Laurence campaigning for adequate housing in inner Melbourne (Holden and Trembath 2008).

Recognizing the need for research to underpin its programmes of policy reform and service provision, the Brotherhood of St Laurence was the first non-government welfare organization in Australia to employ a research officer in 1943. Since then, the employment of social researchers has been an integral feature of the Brotherhood, with many of these research officers being social workers (Holden and Trembath 2008).

Although costing just 3 per cent of the Brotherhood's annual budget, research and advocacy are integral to the wide range of services provided to disadvantaged individuals and communities, including job-seekers, children and families, young people, older people, people with disabilities, newly arrived migrants, and refugees and indigenous Australians (BSL 2012). Consistent with claims that faith-based organizations need skills in being able to 'read' the policy context and engage with policy frameworks (Davis 2009), the more than 600 staff employed by the Brotherhood includes a group of around a dozen research and policy staff (de Leeuw *et al.* 2007) with the director of this group having a joint appointment with the University of Melbourne as Professor in Public Policy (BSL 2012). The Brotherhood recognizes that in order for its work to continue to have an impact on state and national policy, maintaining the highest research standards is crucial; hence its relationship with one of Australia's most prestigious research-intensive universities. In addition to strong and ongoing links with service provision, much of the Brotherhood's research is externally validated through publication in peer-refereed journals and by researchers participating in academic conferences or colloquia (de Leeuw *et al.* 2007). It is thus not surprising that in the areas of poverty and welfare reform it is is widely known and respected not just within but beyond Australia (Davis *et al.* 2008).

In addition to having a culture which considers research and advocacy integral to the organization's identity, the Brotherhood receives a considerable amount of income from sources independent of the state. In 2012, more than a quarter of the annual budget of A$61 million was received from the Brotherhood's social enterprises and fundraising efforts (BSL 2012). With considerable funds of its own, arguably the Brotherhood is less constrained than some other faith-based organizations which are much more highly reliant on state funding and hence may be reluctant to publicly advocate for the communities of service users to which they provide services.

Conclusion

Although some existing faith-based organizations may feel a need to legitimize their position within the welfare state (Angell and Wyller 2006), in the main, faith-based organizations are not clamouring to oust the state from its role in welfare provision (Cnaan *et al.* 1999), and some that in the past have worked in partnership with the state may no longer be prepared to do so (Pipes and Ebaugh 2002). Nevertheless, as faith-based organizations have frequently demonstrated their capacity for service delivery and their credibility (Dinham 2012a), possibly the question is not whether they should be involved in welfare provision, but whether they are able to do so in ways which meet community expectations. As the involvement of religious groups in welfare provision may in part be dependent on their resources (Jupp 2009), the state needs to ensure that faith-based organizations, which are carrying out services on its behalf, or are carrying out services which it recognizes are needed in the community but it is not appropriate for the state to provide these directly, are appropriately resourced and supported (Middlemiss 2006b).

Furness and Gilligan (2012) have argued that rather than asking if faith-based organizations can deliver services more cheaply than the state, the questions which need to be asked by the state include:

> Do FBOs have the capacity to deliver services? Are FBOs able to demonstrate that they are equally or more effective than other organisations in delivering social care and social work services? Is there any added value in a service being provided through a religious group? Will they, for example, mobilise volunteers more effectively? Can FBOs reach and involve socially excluded sections of the community more effectively than others? Will they give equal priority to the needs of their membership and others?
>
> (Furness and Gilligan 2012: 608)

In addition, questions need to be asked as to how the state can ensure that the rights of service users are not violated if the state enters into arrangements with faith-based organizations to provide services on its behalf and whether the needs of the state and faith-based organizations can be met through the participation of faith-based organizations in welfare provision (Swain 2009). Rather than expecting faith-based organizations to become like the state, what is required is a realistic appraisal of the strengths and values of faith-based organizations and the contributions they could make to the communities which they seek to serve (Dinham 2012a).

There may well be discrepancies between theory and practice in respect of the role of faith-based welfare provision (Angell 2010), and many faith-based organizations may need to change direction if they are to remain significant players in the welfare state (Lake 2013), just as the welfare state itself undergoes ongoing changes as well as the society. One aspect of social change which has resulted in questions being raised about the relationship between faith-based organizations and the welfare state concerns the emergence of new faith communities. This issue will be the focus of Chapter 3.

3
FAITH-BASED ORGANIZATIONS IN A MULTI-FAITH SOCIETY

[S]ome have argued that a society which fails to take religion seriously is committing a dereliction of its duty, both to the millions of religious believers who are its citizens and to those who have no faith but who live nevertheless in religiously plural societies. Just as society has a duty to incorporate differences in race and ethnicity, for example, so it is with religious plurality and belief.

(Dinham 2012a: 9)

Introduction

As the above quotation asserts, many would consider it the duty of a society to recognize and respect the diversity of religious traditions of its members. This has variously been used as a justification for providing specific services for members of different faith traditions or as a rationale for all service provision to be secular. The most frequent objection to the existence of faith-based welfare organizations voiced to the author concerns the appropriateness of faith-based providers of welfare services being funded by the state to provide services to the wider community in a multi-faith society. Such objections focus on the differences among religions rather than recognizing that a key imperative in many religions is to provide for those in need (Cnaan *et al.* 1999). On the other hand, for some people of faith, service provision which fails to acknowledge what they consider to be a quintessential aspect of their lives is also problematic.

In countries where regular participation in formal religion is relatively low, there may nevertheless be groups in the community for whom religion is highly significant. For example, although relatively few New Zealanders attend church regularly, religion is very important in the lives of members of the Pasifika communities living in New Zealand with many being regular church attenders, and services need to recognize this (Mafile'o 2009).

Despite often working with service users from a broad array of religions, and in every likelihood doing so with a high degree of competence, some of the research participants in both Australia and Scotland struggled with the question as to what they considered the *role* of faith-based organizations to be in a multi-faith society. Nevertheless, four themes emerged which will be explored in this chapter as possible roles for faith-based providers of welfare services: (1) providing services which meet the specific needs of religious communities; (2) expertise in providing services for immigrants, including refugees and asylum seekers; (3) promoting social cohesion within the wider community; and (4) modelling best practice in social work in responding to issues associated with religious or spiritual issues.

Serving the specific needs of religious communities

Although many faith-based providers of welfare services in countries such as Australia, Canada, New Zealand, the US and the UK now provide services to the wider community, in previous eras faith-based providers essentially existed to provide services to their own communities (Degeneffe 2003). There are however exceptions, particularly involving service providers associated with religious minorities who may struggle with certain aspects of mainstream service delivery. For example, research in the UK into the delivery of hospice services has found that service users experience hospices as reflecting a white Christian ethos into death and dying and not necessarily able to meet the needs of people from other religions (Gatrad and Sheikh 2002; Gatrad *et al.* 2003). Indeed,

> some service users simply will not access services which are open to and widely used by people from other traditions. They seek instead a context which will cater for their own needs in a way which draws on that particular religious tradition. This can also be important where certain constituencies simply will not use a service unless it is delivered to single group constituencies, such as some Muslim women or orthodox Jews, for example.
>
> (Dinham 2012b: 583)

For service users, religious-specific provision may be a particular issue in residential settings, and some residents will have a strong preference for living with co-religionists. While this may represent a desire to be living with others with whom one perceived a shared cultural affinity, it may also be easier to observe dietary and other religious requirements in settings where these do not have to be constantly negotiated as exceptions to standard organizational processes. Faith-specific residential settings can also strengthen communities by bringing together people of the one faith and enabling connections to be made. This may be particularly important for small minority populations. One research participant discussed a short-term residential setting which worked with children in the Jewish community where children 'get to be with some other Jewish kids, it's only a Jewish environment, so there's a real added benefit from the point of view of your community building'.

In addition to providing services to individuals, faith-based organizations may also be better able to engage with some communities than with secular organizations (Kirmani and Khan 2008), and their very existence may form a tangible symbol demonstrating that religious minorities are recognized and considered important (Davie 2012). For example, even though it sometimes works with non-Muslim communities, it has been claimed that Islamic Relief is often at an advantage when working with Muslim refugee communities compared to secular or other faith-based organizations. Following the signing of the Dayton Peace Accords in 1995, many Muslims who had been reluctant to return to Zvornik did so after seeing Islamic Relief being able to work unhindered by the previous conflicts between Bosniaks and Serbs (Kirmani and Khan 2008).

Where migration has seen the arrival of substantial new religious communities, faith-based organizations have emerged to support these communities. This accounts for the establishment and growth of many faith-based organizations associated with non-Christian religions such as Islam, Judaism and Hinduism in traditionally Christian countries in Europe and North America (Clarke 2008). These services are not only able to address demand from community members for services but do so in ways which recognize and respond appropriately to beliefs and practices that are not well understood in the wider community (Gardner 2011). As the manager of a Scottish faith-based organization explained:

> I think potentially it's really important, because I think we've had to learn as an organization about other faiths and the sensitivity around how you value say, Muslim or Judaism as a part of what a family brings to the care of a child and it's been a kind of learning curve for us, because I think you have a sort of Christian standpoint, but actually our society's wider than that. . . . I think what we would say is, 'Because we've believed that being Christian can bring added value to people and what they offer children, we also have been able to translate that to other faiths' and say, 'Well actually, you know, people's commitment to a way of life that's around their religion and their faith, can be wider than Christianity'.

As well as countries which have experienced considerable migration from outside the mainstream religious groups, in societies where there are long-standing religious divisions the necessity for separate provision of services may be considered necessary. For example, during The Troubles in Northern Ireland, the majority of the population refused to use health or social services which had associations, even if just by way of location, with the other religion (McTernan 2003). Similarly, in religiously divided Lebanon, most welfare services are provided by faith-based organizations to their own communities, and government policy has encouraged this (Jawad 2009).

Whether due to migration or pre-existing religious divisions, service providers need a good understanding of the unique cultural factors which may explain how and why community members respond to particular situations as they do. For example, Gilligan and Akhtar (2006) have identified reasons associated with Islamic culture which may explain why far fewer cases of child sexual abuse among Muslim children in Bradford are reported than might be anticipated on the basis of population. However, this is not the same as making an argument for faith-based organizations and it may be necessary to distinguish between concerns specifically associated with religious beliefs and those which just happened to be concentrated within a community. For example, when writing about Muslims in Britain, Hussain noted that neither domestic violence nor forced marriage 'are specifically "Islamic" concerns *per se*, but they do affect significant numbers of Muslims. It could be argued that such issues have more to do with factors such as class, race, education and economics than they do with religion' (Hussain 2012: 626). On the other hand, issues for Muslim communities associated with Islamophobia and the media representation which leads to Muslims feeling marginalized may well be grounds for the existence of faith-specific services (Hussain 2012). Yet since the events of 9/11 in 2001, many Muslim faith-based organizations have found themselves under suspicion of having 'terrorist links' (Kirmani and Khan 2008) and, at a time when perhaps their community most needed them, scapegoating organizations due to their Muslim connections resulting in the closure of some Islamic charities in the United States (Benthall 2007).

Promoting the existence of faith-based organizations may also be a good economic investment. Faith communities, particularly minority ethnic communities, often have access to considerable resources. While this may be used for negative reasons, frequently they have a very positive effect in providing support to community members (Hussain 2012).

Despite their potential to provide services which may be considered more desirable and appropriate to members of faith communities, governments are often reluctant to fund faith-based organizations to provide services exclusively to members of a single faith community. Hence, in Australia, the experience of some faith-based organizations which aim to provide services for their own community is that they don't formally restrict other members of the community using services, but the nature of the service means that few outside the community would ever seek assistance. In Britain however, there has been interest in funding multi-faith initiatives. While these seek to overcome any suggestion of favouritism towards specific religious communities, such initiatives may in fact fail to meet the needs of people of any faith:

> In the end, the multi-faith paradigm proves a conundrum. It has no religious creed, buildings, explicit practices, or formal leaders. It struggles to deliver complex partnership and the broadest of participation. It finds it especially hard to engage with the marginalised, radicalised and extreme whom policy-makers most want to address.
>
> (Dinham 2012b: 586)

Services for immigrants

Global migration increases the need for social and financial assistance (Pettersson 2011); thus supporting immigrants, including refugees and asylum seekers, is a key role for faith-based organizations in many countries. While this may include supporting members of their own religious community, an 'ethic of hospitality' (Wilson 2011: 548), or provision of sanctuary or other forms of caring for strangers, including foreigners or people from other religions, may be found in the teachings of several religions, including Christianity, Judaism, Islam and Buddhism (Ives *et al.* 2010; Snyder 2011). As an Australian Christian social worker observed:

> I guess they are very much minority groups aren't they. I guess it's about survival and not losing their identity. I don't know enough about other religions to know how much outreach they do, whether that's part of their faith or not. It's part of the Christian faith to be reaching out and giving like to whoever rather than just looking after ourselves.

When such services are provided across the boundaries of religious traditions, faith-based organizations may view this as opportunities to develop meaningful relationships with people from other religions (Eby *et al.* 2011), taking note that historically this wasn't always the case. As another research participant commented:

> I'll say wars against Catholicism, and of the medieval times and everything like that, I think it's actually important that there are organizations out there that promote the tolerance of different faiths, because otherwise, you do risk that if you have a different religion that you, if people aren't used to it, then they tend to become more intolerant.

As in other areas in which faith-based organizations provide services, provision of services to immigrants partly reflects perceived needs which are not being met by the state or by other providers and the available resources to meet these needs (Wilson 2011). However, as one Australian social worker noted, many of the challenges for faith-based organizations when working with immigrants are the same as for non-faith-based organizations:

> Well, we're working with some asylum seekers and that has been challenging in that they have very poor language skills, so we've had to organize and pay for interpreters, things like that. But anybody would experience that. That's the challenge that any agency would have.

Assisting newcomers to settle and provide them with relevant support has been referred to as 'the cuddlesome face of religion valued by governments' (Snyder 2011: 570). Such is the reputation of faith-based organizations in this field of practice that in the US, six of the ten voluntary agencies contracted by the Office of Refugee Resettlement are faith-based agencies with Jewish or Christian affiliations (Ives *et al.* 2010). Provided they are assured that the faith-based organization will not be checking their immigration status and reporting on their status to the state (Pipes and Ebaugh 2002), involvement in religious welfare organizations can address feelings of alienation for members of religious and ethnic minorities. Religious groups which have experienced persecution may have developed their own services, being wary of what was offered by the broader community. In Australia, this was true for both Catholics and Jews in earlier generations (Jupp 2009). Muslim youth in Sweden experience a sense of alienation and being positioned as 'other' within Swedish society, but also expectations from non-Muslims that they can explain aspects of Islam. In this context, membership of a Muslim youth organization provided opportunities both for solidarity and for learning more about Islam (Karlsson Miganti 2010).

However, many faith-based organizations are not content just to be a 'cuddlesome face of religion' and consider their role to also include challenging public discourses and policies which have further contributed to the marginalization and oppression of immigrant communities. This can involve seeking:

> to *unsettle* any established population attitudes and policies which contribute to the difficulties faced by newcomers. . . . These activities are issue-centred and concentrate on the public voicing of concerns, transforming attitudes, advocacy and policy intervention.
>
> (Snyder 2011: 572)

This often involves advocacy (Jupp 2009), and faith-based organizations have been highly critical of government policies concerning refugees and asylum seekers in many countries. At the same time, faith-based organizations also model ways of working with immigrant communities. For example, it has been argued that when faith-based organizations appear to be more open than the state to employing immigrants and integrating them into society, other sectors of society may become more open to including them (Fokas 2006). One Australian social worker spoke of her experiences in working for a faith-based organization that very deliberately sought to recruit staff from other faith traditions:

> My experience of the faith-based agencies I've worked in would be that it's not limited to anyone because of their faith and I've seen increasing attempts to recruit other faiths to be staff members, to be volunteers. I actually think there's been a lot more affirmative action around that and I know at one point towards the end of my time at [faith-based organization], my manager at the time was actively marketing the fact that we had volunteers from other faiths, in fact almost to the point where that was marketed more than the other diversity in the volunteer base.

Undoubtedly many faith-based organizations do excellent work with immigrants and immigrant communities. Nevertheless, there is a tendency to conflate ethnicity and religion although in reality the relationship between these is complex (Dinham and Lowndes 2008), and hence being based in a religious tradition doesn't necessarily qualify organizations to do this work. Furthermore, people who have been oppressed on the basis of their religion may not be receptive to receiving services which they perceive to be aligned to the religion of their oppressors (Al-Krenawi and Graham 2008). In some cases immigrants may have an antipathy towards any faith-based organization or any faith-based organization from outside their own religious tradition of which they have no knowledge. Both Australian and Scottish social workers observed a reluctance among some immigrant groups to use services run by faith-based organizations for the wider community. A typical comment was:

> We're losing a lot of clients, we're not supporting so I think there's a large group out there that we're not providing support because maybe they think due to their cultural beliefs or religion; they think [organization] isn't the right organization for them.

Promoting social cohesion

In response to increasing social tensions and divisions among different religious and ethnic communities during recent years, policy-makers in the

UK have explicitly sought to forge links with the faith-based welfare sector (Baker 2012) in the belief that this is an effective way of building social capital and enhancing social cohesion (Furbey *et al.* 2005). Similarly, it has been claimed that the Lebanese government has regarded supporting religious organizations to develop welfare services as a strategy for building harmony in a country where religious divides run deep (Jawad 2009). Such initiatives reflect that most religions 'have core principles that can motivate bridge-building and link-making through community service, cooperation, peace-making, the pursuit of social justice, and the acceptance of others' (Furbey *et al.* 2005: 8). In terms of social cohesion, many faith-based welfare organizations actually model ways of working which acknowledge and respect different religious traditions and some actively encourage staff from other religions to share key facets of their faith, such as about religious festivals. Research participants from a number of Australian faith-based organizations made observations similar to the following:

> because we work with people of all faith backgrounds, we employ people of all faith backgrounds. So I would hope that it would mean that we could respect that in a much more authentic way than just a lip service sort of way. And I think that it does provide the opportunity to open up dialogues. So very rich dialogues would be here. . . . I would hope that's a more respectful way that because we come from a Christian perspective, that we can be much more respectful of people of other faiths than if we were not faith based.

Rather than attempting to homogenize different religious traditions, accepting the diversity is an important step along the road to social cohesion (Dinham 2009). However, establishing dialogue doesn't guarantee that cohesion will follow and a degree of scepticism about this strategy may well be warranted (Jawad 2009), particularly if it assumes a capacity for the leaders of religious communities to take a lead in promoting cohesion within and among communities which may not exist (Paton *et al.* 2009). Moreover, religious communities may themselves be characterized by diversity and struggle to achieve internal cohesion, let alone cohesion with other religions. For example, Barise (2005) has estimated that the Muslim community in Canada included members born in more than 60 countries with great diversity in respect of life experiences and welfare needs. Hence, while governments or other funding bodies often want to link with the faith-based sector for ideological reasons such as enhancing social cohesion, faith-based organizations may choose to partner with government for pragmatic reasons, i.e. needing funds or other resources to run programmes for which the organization has identified a need (Furbey *et al.* 2005).

In the minds of some policy-makers, closely associated with promoting social cohesion is building social capital. Hence, faith-based services are favoured by policy-makers who want to use the resources of, and strengthen links with, faith communities (Dinham and Lowndes 2009). At the most basic level this may simply be the ability to enable different communities to meet through the shared use of space. As one Australian social worker explained:

> This space is used on other days for the Somali population, there's the Somali meeting here on Tuesdays, and we have the Aboriginal men meet up in the hall and do their art work up there. I mean, it really is, they're working towards making it more open and getting more people from all walks of life and faith traditions involved, and that's something that they do very well, and they're very welcoming in that sense. So I guess I don't see how that's, they're not exclusive, in terms of, they're very welcoming.

At an organizational level, faith-based organizations can also work together to achieve goals that may be more difficult for individual organizations. As a Scottish social worker explained:

> I don't think we would ever be as ardent to say that we would understand completely where other faiths are at in terms of their understanding of people. You know you're only able to respond to that but I think the care for people and the care for people as beings – I don't know if I'm making myself very clear here – we have a common thread there and we should be able to work together. But you also – I think in society in Britain, you know, different faith groups can work together as a pressure on local government and on government, you know, about meeting the needs of people. That where government and local government may be driven by economic policies that maybe you know kind of not looking so much at welfare issues. So I think we should be able to work together.

In bringing together diverse communities, the hope is that each will benefit. In making connections between the minority Muslim community and the wider Australian community in her local area, another of the research participants reflected:

> I don't think you can stop the tide of people moving around the world and moving into different communities and influencing different communities. I like to think that some of the Muslim people around here will influence our young men and hopefully they'll stop drinking because that's one of their rules, if only, and I just hope it's not going to be the other way round.

However, the social capital in some faith-based organizations may not be what is considered desirable to emulate if it is inequalities, for example, where men and older people dominate the priority setting (Furbey *et al.* 2005). Furthermore, despite

> the dangers of the celebratory tone of some official policy documents
> . . . . Faith communities face important internal and external obstacles
> in fulfilling any potential that they might have as sources and gener-
> ators of social capital. They may themselves also *be* obstacles to the
> outward-looking and enriching social networks.
>
> (Furbey *et al.* 2005: 3)

As one research participant explained:

> To me faith is the important word. Religiosity is where we've all gone
> wrong. So I think when we've become too tied up in our own particular
> denomination, and perhaps even our own particular religion we have
> sometimes become quite restricted in the way that we want to express
> the work that we're doing, and also judgemental of the, of our
> neighbour who may also be doing the work of justice in our community.
> So to me, look, if people are working out of principles of love and
> justice and respect, and their finding strength in, to me God is present
> in that context.

It is thus ironic that policy processes which seek to promote cohesion can be borne out of intolerance and disrespect. British author Adam Dinham raises the very real question as to whether it is realistic for governments to have seemingly participated in the vilification of some religions and then expecting that those organizations associated with those religions would willingly cooperate to promote government policies:

> The turn to faith as a potential problem is quite understandable in the
> post-9/11 context. But it presents policy with a conflict. How are we
> to reconcile the instrumentalization of faiths in civil society with their
> vilification as proponents of terror within it? Faiths will not withstand
> being cast as both heroes and villains for long. It is a position which
> can only fragment and polarize.
>
> (Dinham 2009: 193)

Modelling best practice

When faith-based organizations develop a reputation for excellent practice, they will attract service users from beyond their own religious community, and may pride themselves on doing so. Social workers in both Scotland and

Australia spoke about the need to practise with a high degree of cultural sensitivity. In the words of one:

> There's a lot of emphasis on professional development to be able to practise in culturally sensitive ways and to understand and respect people of all different backgrounds. I think our existence is more about our value statement than who we are and our intention . . . [to] provide these services because of something we believe in.

Hence one role which faith-based organizations can play is in modelling good practice in working with people from diverse religious traditions. This involves an openness to dialogue with other faiths, as explained by an Australian social worker:

> So I think it's around values, relationship and if you've got the right values you enter into a relationship and it becomes embracing or a symbiotic relationship where you learn from the other. Each learns some . . . I think we as an agency because of our values would be open to embracing other cultures, other religions through the commonality rather than the difference between them.

However, even for organizations where this is a priority, it may nevertheless be an ongoing challenge. Members of the wider religious community or service users may be far less open to anti-discriminatory practice than social workers employed in faith-based organizations, as one research participant recounted:

> Well, I think the challenge really comes down then to being the uncon-ditional love aspect of it and non-discriminatory, non-judgemental, which I think is probably quite challenging because particularly the older generation, so the early baby boomers, or whatever the genera-tion was before that, my parents' generation, can be quite black and white and judgemental and racist.

Efforts to avoid being regarded as judgemental at times result in staff members in faith-based organizations avoiding having explicit conversations about matters associated with religion. Not discussing religion also avoids any claims of proselytizing which might be construed as a lack of sensitivity towards people of other faiths. Rather, they may 'emphasize values common across a range of faith traditions, such as justice and compassion' (Wilson 2011: 553) rather than concepts specific to a particular religion. On the other hand, the issue of religion may be more on the practice agenda in faith-based organizations, encouraging social workers to consider whether there may be religious or spiritual dimensions which need to be identified (Furness and Gilligan 2010b). In the words of one social worker:

> It's an interesting question isn't it? I think the lack of any faith or any kind of belief in a transcendent God, I don't know how to identify it, you feel there's something missing for them, the sense of hope or purpose or meaning or any support from outside themselves, there's certainly a difference, I'm not quite sure how to name that, you just feel it with people. I think you feel a certain sadness that that's not there, it doesn't become an issue with the counselling but it's something I feel is sad for them, there's something missing.

Nevertheless, faith-based organizations may also be venues in which the question of whether religion might be a resource service which users can call upon may be raised (Furness and Gilligan 2010b). As the previous speaker also said:

> We've had people from almost every religion imaginable here. It's useful actually, if they've got some kind of religion or some kind of faith in God, it's often helpful for them. If they haven't they haven't, sometimes they're missing a dimension to their lives that could be helpful to them in the circumstances they're in. They can make more sense out of what's going on and sometimes they draw strength and they draw some meaning that gives them some strength if they have some faith, doesn't make any difference which one.

It may well be surprising to many people that a faith-based organization was more interested in the question of whether a service user had religious beliefs or a faith community that provided support or from which they could draw strength, than in pushing the religious beliefs associated with the organization (Dinham 2012a). Hence faith-based organizations may well be able to demonstrate to the broader welfare sector that best practice in social work doesn't include forgoing asking questions of service users which recognize the holding of religious beliefs as a potentially valid resource.

In Australia, as in other countries, some funding streams invite consortiums, rather than individual organizations to bid for the right to run particular programmes. Although it has been suggested that organizations from different religious traditions may find it easier to work together in fighting campaigns against policy than in providing programmes or services (Furbey and Macey 2005), faith-based organizations do often partner with a range of other organizations in such arrangements, and if they are recognized as being efficient and effective providers of services, they will be sought-after partners in service provision (Kirmani and Khan 2008). In addition, by being members of multi-agency consortiums, once programme protocols and practice guidelines are developed, faith-based organizations have the potential to share their best practice in respect of dealing with matters associated with religion and spirituality in a multi-faith society. However, this potential can only be realized if faith-based organizations involved in such consortia do not place a strong emphasis on religious conversion (Benedetti 2006). Furthermore, while consortias including faith-based organizations can be very effective in achieving their aims (Ivereigh 2009), apparent tolerance of faith-based organizations associated with other religions or no religion can represent more of a pragmatic truce in order to ensure that resources are obtained by a community than a genuine desire for collaboration (Fiddian-Qasmiyeh 2011).

Conclusion

This chapter has outlined four potential roles for faith-based organizations in multi-faith societies. These are: (1) as a provider of services which meet the specific needs of religious communities; (2) as a provider of services for immigrant communities; (3) promoting social cohesion; and (4) modelling best practice in social work in responding to issues associated with religious or spiritual issues. This is not necessarily an exhaustive list and possibly reflects the research methodology. While rationales can be established which support each of these four roles for faith-based welfare organizations, none of these is straightforward and each is subject to a number of caveats as outlined above. Furthermore, it is important not to stereotype faith-based groups (Furbey and Macey 2005), and the capacity of individual organizations to play each of these roles will vary considerably.

Even if roles for faith-based organizations in multi-faith societies can be established, questions remain as to how much these should be supported, particularly if that support involves public funding. Different countries have varying histories and predilections as to the funding of faith-based organizations versus other non-government organizations or government instrumentalities in respect of different aspects of social work practice (Crisp 2013). First, how do you fund some faith groups without antagonizing others who might have similar claims for funding (Ahmed *et al.* 2009)? This applies both to groups from different religions as well as competing groups associated with the same religion. Second, if it is not feasible to grant all religions equal recognition, how does the state provide adequate recognition to all, especially minority religions, and ensure that the needs of those communities are met (Parekh 2009)?

It is perhaps inevitable that the existence of contemporary faith-based organizations will raise difficult questions for individuals, organizations and whole societies, and some more of these questions will be considered in further chapters. In recognition that there are various stakeholders, often with diverse perspectives, Chapter 4 will identify some of the key stakeholders in faith-based welfare provision.

4

STAKEHOLDERS

Faith groups may also find it hard to express religious values, beliefs and principles in a more secularised context due to fear of sounding 'a bit weird' or because they themselves take them for granted. A member of the Salvation Army who was interviewed highlighted a need to adopt a more 'secularised language' in this context, using terms such as 'honesty, tolerance and the importance of relationships', as opposed to more instinctively Christian language of 'grace, peace, joy and love'. This led to concerns about what is 'lost in translation'.

(Chapman 2009: 212)

How does a Catholic agency become 'bi-lingual', that is, both theologically literate and professionally literate, such that the same reality can be expressed in two different ways without compromise to either theological or professional discourse?

What is the right balance between these two 'languages'? Which 'language' is best to be used? When? How? With whom? And by whom?

(Ranson 2008: 91)

Introduction

As both of the above quotations indicate, faith-based organizations need to be 'bi-lingual' in order to engage in discourses with diverse stakeholders. All social welfare agencies, including those run by the state, have a range of stakeholders, including staff, service users, funders, competing organizations and members of the wider community (Ozanne and Rose 2013). However, in many faith-based organizations there is the additional complexity of the religious community, which itself may have a wide diversity of members with different perspectives about the welfare services which the community auspices and the relationship between the religious and welfare services provided (Dinham 2009). While some stakeholders will be closely connected with the local communities where services are provided, other stakeholders may have little or no connection (Middlemiss 2006b) and the professionalization of service delivery can have the effect of dismantling links between religious communities and the services they auspice (Dinham 2009).

In addition to having various and often diverse perspectives, stakeholders may be numerous. For example, welfare provision by the Church of Sweden includes the employment of 1,200 social welfare professionals in parishes across the country which is funded by a tax levy on church members (Hansson 2006) paid by the 80 per cent or more of Swedes who consider themselves to be members of the Church of Sweden (Leis-Peters 2009). In addition to staff, faith-based welfare organizations often have substantial numbers of volunteers, who may outnumber paid staff, as well as numerous service users, many of whom retain a keen interest in the organization after their formal involvement has ceased (Holden and Trembath 2008).

Many faith-based welfare organizations begin as a small project or the idea of an individual or group of people, only later becoming a formal organization which employs professional staff, including social workers. As they evolve and new stakeholders emerge, tensions can readily surface within faith-based organizations (Jeavons and Cnaan 1997). While recognizing that groups of stakeholders are themselves often not homogeneous and that membership of these groups is not always discrete, this chapter will consider some key stakeholders in faith-based organizations, i.e. the religious or faith community, the professional welfare community, funders, service users, the wider community, and the board of management which often acts as the common interface point between the various groups of stakeholders.

Religious community

What frequently differentiates religious communities from other community groups which recognize the need for new welfare services is having assets, including staff and buildings, which may be deployed to facilitate the establishment of such services (Garland *et al.* 2008). However, religious communities may also have views as to what types of services they are prepared to support, with perceived compatibility with their overall mission as critical (Fagan *et al.* 2010), especially when it comes to making decisions as to what they are not prepared to lend their name and/or resources to (Cnaan *et al.* 1999; Leis-Peters 2006). For example, in the case of one small Australian faith-based organization, staff were initially able to be employed only because the members of a local church were able to provide some funding:

> In the days before we got the latest bit of philanthropic funding, they were basically throwing money in the hat to keep us alive, and ticking along for a few months while we desperately tried to get some money.

The religious or faith community often comprises both the broader community of people who identify with a particular religion, as well as the formal organization and religious hierarchy. The hierarchy itself may be local or at a distance with oversight of communities and programmes at a regional, national or even international level. In respect of high-level organizations where these exist, denominations or dioceses or other metagroups of religious communities vary considerably in both structure and resources. For example, there are approximately 13,000 parishes, organized into 44 dioceses in England of the Church of England, compared to a single office to support the work of Zoroastrians right across Europe (Dinham 2009). Some faith groupings are loose federations which provide advice and support to relatively autonomous local congregations or communities whereas in others, the central organization is more akin to head office issuing directives to local branch offices (Torry 2005). This not only relates to religious worship but also to the organization of welfare efforts. For example, the Church of Finland has a requirement that every parish employs a worker who provides welfare services on behalf of the Church (Jokela 2011).

While there may be agreement that the church or religious community should be involved in some form of welfare, this does not necessarily mean that all stakeholders believe such enterprises should employ professional social workers. Rather, some may posit that the faith community should provide what professionals cannot (Middlemiss 2006b). For example, despite the extensive welfare undertakings of the Church of Finland, there is a lack of consensus among Finns as to what role the Church should play in providing welfare services. Whereas some believe that the Church should provide more spiritual and less welfare services, others think that both should be provided equally (Pessi 2010), and the job descriptions of church welfare workers can be a mix of professional welfare and ostensibly religious duties (Jokela 2011). Such tensions may be observed in many different religions in varying countries such that 'With few exceptions, most religious groups engage in social and community service as a means to witness their faith, fulfill religious teaching and beliefs, or simply "do good" for others in the community' (Cnaan *et al.* 1999: 300).

Those members of the religious community who envisage that a key role of faith-based organizations includes the religious conversion of service users will often be pragmatic and recognize that 'The desire to save souls and spread the Gospel solely through social services provision has proved to be both ineffective and too expensive' (Cnaan *et al.* 1999: 300). But that does not necessarily dampen their desire for this to occur and social workers have to deal with this tension on a daily basis. As an Australian social worker employed by an agency which is part of an evangelical church remarked:

> Luckily, I've got very good management, who acknowledge that we do work with a diverse range of clients, so there are going to be clients who've had negative experiences with the church, who actually have difficulty accepting assistance from a church-based organization. So we tend to alert them at the start that ... the [organization] would prefer to see everybody in church, but as we're a mental health organization, we won't force that.

Furthermore, emphasizing conversion can hinder members of the religious community from recognizing other reasons for supporting welfare initiatives, as was observed by a research participant who had studied theology as well as social work:

> When I say 'they', it's a generalized statement, but a number of them struggle because they see their main purpose is to win souls for the kingdom and they fail to see what we can actually be Jesus to people who are just in need, without having to get them into Heaven or whatever.

Religious communities who take seriously the challenges and opportunities that emerge from running welfare services may actually open themselves up to the risk of changing their thinking and practices:

> Working in the field of social services today does not only mean adapting to the ruling conditions, but also being influenced by them. This raises the question of how the church changes if it is running professionalized and specialized welfare services with financial management.
>
> (Leis-Peters 2006: 111)

Yet it must be recognized that many religious communities have adapted and continue to adapt in response to the needs of the communities with which they work. In discussing the involvement of Catholic religious orders in welfare provision, a social worker commented:

> those orders that are beside the church and are recognized by the church too, is that they are very practical, down-to-earth sort of people

who don't be bothered with a lot of the sort of ivory tower stuff of the church hierarchy but who are practical and would do what needs to be done for the welfare of the person.

The hierarchies of religious communities may have their own understandings of 'what needs to be done for the welfare of the people' based on religious teachings rather than contemporary social work theory. Religious leaders appointed on the basis of their spiritual leadership may find themselves responsible for managing the work of all employees, including those appointed to social welfare positions, although they may have little or no expertise in either social work or management (Andersen 2004), or little knowledge of the day-to-day workings of welfare programmes under their control (Cnaan *et al.* 1999). A not untypical scenario described by an Australian social worker was that:

> as you get higher up, so there's a number of levels of management and a lot of those levels of management are filled by [religious officials], some who have no social work experience or training whatsoever. So when I started with the [organization] . . . the person who came in to be [senior church official responsible for organization] had come straight from the church ministry and had no idea. Wasn't social work trained, had no idea of social work. He was a nice person and he did a reasonably good job, but he didn't have any of that training.

Consequently, it can be extremely frustrating for social workers employed in such organizations. Another research participant described the experience of working in an organization in which social work expertise was valued less highly than religious beliefs when it came to strategic decision-making:

> One of the major obstacles, which I said at the start, is about people being in the hierarchy at the top making decisions in which they have no experience of dealing with people in different groups. That's really annoying because what it does is that it flows down the ladder and so it puts a perception out there that there's a limit on how much we can or cannot do. So in the welfare sector, do they have a role? I think so, but I believe they need to be very well structured.

Arguably one of the tasks of such religious officials is to ensure that the needs of the religious community are addressed, whatever these are perceived to be. As mentioned in Chapter 1, some have suggested that the change of name of the Catholic diocesan welfare agencies in Australia served to endear these services to the local Catholic communities. Religious communities often provide a large support base of donors, volunteers, resources as well as moral support for the various welfare services with which they associate themselves (Holden and Trembath 2008). For example, a not untypical scenario in some Australian faith-based organizations is that:

> people will leave bequests from time to time. . . . and donors, Christmas appeals, all that sort of stuff. . . . But like at Christmas time here, it never fails in December. We had numerous lovely [religious denomination] people from around here who would turn up and they'll either give us a monetary donation, they'll give us a hamper, they'll come in and say, 'What can we do?' So it's, there's the individual goodwill person here, through to the donor organization who decides to give 10 grand to [organization] on June 30th. It might be for their tax deduction but it's really helpful it comes our way. Also, and they give because they believe that this is a faith-based organization and it aligns with their faith perspective.

The overall contributions from members of religious communities towards welfare services is frequently considerable. For example, it has been estimated that if social service programmes provided by local congregations in the US city of Philadelphia were to be replaced by the state or by other providers, this would result in a cost of $250 million per annum (Cnaan and Newman 2010). Similarly, in the Canadian province of Manitoba, the Salvation Army alone provided $89 million worth of services in 2005 (Schwartz *et al.* 2008). Although the Salvation Army often actively attracts funding to subsidize its work, it nevertheless often puts in considerable additional resources of its own into programmes. These are not isolated examples of religious communities with a particular penchant for providing social services, and arguably, in many regions across the world and across a wide range of religious groupings, setting aside considerable funds for the provision of welfare services is the norm. Nevertheless, members of religious communities may overestimate the extent to which they financially support welfare services carried out under their auspice. As a social worker in a Scottish faith-based organization which receives a tiny proportion of its annual income from the church explained, 'It's always been like that actually and it's bizarre because you know you go to the big Church jamboree kind of meetings where we have our brochure and say "Oh, we fund you so well", actually you don't'.

While it has been suggested that even a small monetary contribution by a religious community can have a significant impact in terms of forging the identity of a faith-based organization (Vanderwoerd 2004), financial dependence upon outside sources can result in professional welfare services losing contact with the faith communities which have supported their establishment:

> The trend toward professionalization of services . . . while required by our funders, may also have contributed to a certain disengagement

between human service agencies and the lay community that makes up the broader church population. . . . The life of the school, hospital or welfare agency appear to be quite separated from what have been traditional communities of the faithful.

(Quinlan 2008: 47)

Hence, in religious groups where welfare services are centralized rather than being provided by local congregations, faith-based organizations may intentionally seek to establish links with the local members of the religious community. While this may occur with the expectation of attracting money or volunteers, in a residential setting it may also be about enhancing the sense of social connectedness of service users. An Australian social worker employed in a residential setting suggested:

I think someone should come here. People, they should come visit, make their presence known, and talk to people. . . .
And who do you mean by 'they'?
People from the [religious denomination], yeah. I believe they should come and see us. More of a visible presence maybe. But then again, maybe they want to stay in the background. It's hard to say, isn't it? I mean, I don't know what they actually want from us.

Interestingly, despite having been employed by a large faith-based organization for many years, this social worker did not consider that she had any contact with 'the church' as she understood it. Her comments also raise the question of to what extent, once they have become professionalized, do faith-based organizations seek more than donations and moral support from the wider religious community?

When they do invest in services, whether or not individuals are active participants in their religious community, they may take an interest in, and have opinions about, services provided by and for their community. Jewish communities are often concentrated in small areas, such that one-sixth of the Jewish population in the United Kingdom live in a single London borough where many of the services provided specifically for the Jewish community are located (Valins 2011). A similar situation exists in Australia, where Jewish communities predominantly live in a small cluster of suburbs in large cities and many members of the community have links with the various services provided for their community. An Australian social worker noted, 'it's a very tight community. . . . So in that sense everything you do in the Jewish community if it touches one Jewish person it can touch a whole lot more very quickly.' Like the staff in an Islamic clinic in Egypt who felt they could approach board members when they were praying together at the mosque (Clark 1995), members of Jewish communities in Australia often feel they can approach staff and board members of Jewish organizations at any time and not just within the organizational context. As a social worker working in the Jewish community in an Australian city explained:

> They lived in the same suburb so people saw one another, they could talk about it. So if something happened that wasn't good people would find that out very quickly. And plus there's the Jewish newspaper which, you know, a lot of people from the Jewish community read.

In response to the high degree of interest and investment in services, organizations working with the Jewish community will in turn be highly responsive to what they perceive to be the needs of the community. As the previous speaker went on to explain:

> Everything we did at [organization] was actually tied to the values and beliefs about what we offered and we always had to ask those questions if we were designing a new service. We had to ask: how does this fit with the Jewish community? . . . And a sense of that there was always something you could kind of look to and think: does it meet our values and beliefs?

Nevertheless, the opinions of community members as to aims of welfare services associated with their community, and the roles of professional staff which they employ, may be limited and unrealistic. Furthermore, there may be little understanding in the wider religious community as to the actual costs of professionally running welfare services (Netting 1982). Large faith-based organizations may receive little or no recurrent funding from the religious communities which may have founded them and continue to auspice (Smith and Sosin 2001), and are instead funded by the state and must comply with the expectations which come with state funding (Leis-Peters 2006). Alternatively, the work of social workers may be confused with roles of an ostensibly religious nature (Northern 2009); one Australian social worker found himself in an organization where there had been an expectation that social workers would participate in general fundraising efforts for the religious community:

> Before I came to the organization I knew of a lady who went there before me, she's gone now, and she was saying . . . that they were actually encouraged to go and doorknock appeal on the weekend, on their time off. It was expected that all the colleagues would do that. Now that doesn't happen anymore, but there's been a change, they seem to have done a reassessment after a few staff didn't like it.

It is perhaps inevitable that at times faith-based providers of professional welfare services will be forced to consider compromises. An example of this is the case of Catholic adoption agencies in Britain which is explored in Chapter 6. While some faith-based organizations have the resources and sufficient goodwill of the community to continue to provide services on their own terms, withdrawing from service delivery is a decision which religious communities may be forced to make.

Professional community

Just as the religious community incorporates a number of players, so too does the professional community associated with faith-based welfare services. These include social workers and other professional staff within faith-based organizations, other key organizations in the sector, as well as regulatory bodies that may have perspectives which conflict with those emerging from the religious community. For the professional community especially, having a religious tradition may lead to constraints not necessarily experienced outside the faith-based sector (La Barbera 1992).

The professionalization of social work during the twentieth century led to changing relationships between social workers and those whom they viewed as non-professionals, including clergy, volunteers and board members, and whose contributions they often readily devalued (Scales 2011). In particular, trained social workers were often critical of charity fuelled by what they regarded as sentimentality rather than being based on so-called rational or scientific assessments (Kunzel 1988). Yet the reality of some faith-based organizations is that social workers do work alongside volunteers and a blurring of roles may result (Netting *et al.* 2005).

A consequence of the professionalization of the workforce in the latter part of the twentieth century has been that increasingly social workers were being employed from outside the faith community in many faith-based organizations, including some of the organizations with which research participants were associated in both Australia and Scotland. This results in the professional workforce having less of an understanding of the faith base to services provided. While the following comment was made about Catholic services in Australia, similar comments may be said to apply in many other faith-based welfare services in different countries:

> Our agencies now operate with a new workforce. . . . Importantly, in addition to being non-Catholic and non-practising, our workforce is less likely to have had the educational and cultural experiences that might engender some prior understanding of Catholic life and culture. In this context we cannot even assume that some of our very basic assumptions will immediately resonate in the lives of people who make up our workforce.
>
> (Quinlan 2008: 51)

When religious beliefs clash with their professional values (Reid 2008), it has been proposed that the skills of reflective practice and critical dialogue may assist social workers to work through the differences, and if these cannot be resolved, at least to better understand the issues (Green 2010). While social workers should be reluctant to adopt ways of working which are inconsistent with the values and principles of social work, at the same time they need to ensure that approaches they reject on the basis of any religious affiliation have also been properly considered. As Gilligan has warned:

> Any faith-based approach needs to be analysed and evaluated, not only by those responsible for the regulation of social work, but, perhaps more especially, by those adopting it and those on the receiving end of its services. It may provide exactly what is needed in particular circumstances, either because of or despite its faith characteristics, but, at the same time, it may fail to do so, for the same reasons.
>
> (Gilligan 2010: 70)

Individual welfare organizations seldom work in isolation and often work in partnership with a wide range of other services, in addition to being a source of referrals and organizations to which faith-based organizations refer service users. These organizations will no doubt have their own criteria by which they judge faith-based organizations with whom they work. Also, faith-based organizations will often be well regarded by the wider professional community. As one Australian social worker commented about her organization:

> I think [organization] is known as an organization that will go the extra mile. . . . I think we have some sort of pride in that. Some pride in the agency that we work with the hardest ones, the ones others have given up on and keep on trying to break through with the person's problems.

For faith-based organizations, strategic alliances with other like-minded organizations may be crucial in order to remain viable (Jawad 2009). But as one research participant from a very small faith-based organization reflected, choice of partners is critical:

> I think it's going to be very difficult for them to remain viable, just being able to source funding, and that's why, for example, with us, we're trying to be pragmatic about we're going to have to try and pick a larger organization like [organization] who are like-minded . . . their values are more akin to our values, because the danger is that when you link in to a large organization, you get gobbled up, and what makes you you, or what makes your organization unique, or special, can get gobbled up by another agency.

However, competitive funding arrangements can also limit cooperative working arrangements between faith-based organizations and other service providers for faith-based organizations of all sizes. In response to the question of whether other agencies had particular expectations of faith-based organizations, it was suggested by a social worker who had worked for a large faith-based organization in Australia that:

> Other organizations may not see them differently at all. They may see them as being the same as them. I don't think that's helped by competitive tendering these days, because we compete against each other.

Funders

Running welfare organizations which employ professional social workers costs money. While there are some religious communities that have the capacity to pay all salaries and other essential costs from their own resources and from any fees paid by service users, many seek support from government or other charitable funding organizations who may be willing to support their work (Northern 2009). At the same time as faith-based organizations may be seeking external funding, funding organizations typically have their own agendas, which may include the belief that faith-based organizations are able to deliver services more cost-efficiently than other categories of service providers (Angell and Wyller 2006). A study of faith-based welfare organizations in Alberta, Canada found that 79 per cent had sought government funds in the previous six years, and 69 per cent of these agencies regarded government funding as being positive for their agencies, and were able to work collaboratively with their government funders (Hiemstra 2002).

Entering into funding agreements may require compromises from both faith-based organizations and funders. Funding organizations may be more inclined towards faith-based organizations whose welfare activities are quite distinct from ostensibly religious actitivies (Dinham 2009) and be suspicious of faith-based organizations where such a distinction is less apparent (Furbey et al. 2005). Nevertheless, they may be willing to overlook some religious aspects of programming, and at the same time faith-based organizations may move in new directions which are in opposition to the organization's ethos (Langer 2003). An Australian social worker made the observation that:

> I think the lure of funding of programmes and growth, I won't want to name names on this one, but I see some other faith-based agency doing programmes that I wouldn't be prepared to work in and wouldn't go near with a barge-pole. I don't agree with how the funding originates. I don't agree with the whole intent of the programme. I don't commit

to that policy direction that the government might be making, so I just wouldn't go near it.

Receipt of funding may also require faith-based organizations to play down any explicit expression of their religious beliefs and principles (Langer 2003; Unruh and Sider 2005) or agree not to speak out against the policy position of their funders (Lake 2013). However, while their employers may be willing to make such compromises with funders, this doesn't necessarily sit so easily with employee social workers:

> I think this is perhaps an issue as more of the faith-based agency funding is connected with contracts with the government and clauses within those contracts that might preclude them from advocating and making comment about government policies and programmes. But I think that we should retain some degree of autonomy, so that we can do advocacy, so that we can fundraise and do other than just what we're funded for, but really still remain on the edge and looking for those gaps in services where disadvantaged people are trying to make the most and might require some additional support.

On the other hand, being willing to forgo some advocacy may be perceived by social workers as essential both to ensure ongoing funding of programmes which will benefit service users and also to secure their own employment. As one social worker noted, it is 'very easy to be sucked into recurrent funding that eases that issue of will a programme be able to exist next year and helps you with planning, yeah definitely. It makes you viable to know what income you can expect'.

Ongoing funding may be less of a certainty than it is perceived to be and programmes which may once have attracted funds may lose their pulling power over time (Lake 2013). Furthermore, despite often being favoured over other community organizations by funders (Middlemiss 2006b), faith-based organizations in many countries are increasingly being required to apply for funding through competitive processes, rather than being able to point to track records demonstrating capacity to provide services (Leis-Peters 2006).

Concerned that government funding will curtail their programmes and ways of working, some faith-based organizations choose to forgo government funding (Hiemstra 2002). Funding guidelines may limit the amount of discretion which can be exercised or require faith-based organizations to treat all service users equitably (Rogers 2009). External funding can bring new expectations that programmes will be evaluated (Phillips *et al.* 2008), and organizations with a strong religious emphasis may have different definitions of effectiveness than those recognized by funding bodies or other partners/stakeholders (Sherr *et al.* 2009). However, working in collaboration with government and other funding organizations can also provide opportunities to help shape the policy agenda. One of the Australian social workers commented that:

> We have become more and more professionalized and more and more reliant on government for all the reasons that you and I know about, and that has its pros and cons. And there's still some smallish church organizations who refuse to take government funding because they don't want to be strapped up in that. But I think if, because we work with government that we've got to continue to advocate for our clients and our client base and participate in that debate, and keep participating in the justice debate.

Participating in debates may require faith-based organizations to challenge funders as to whether their expectations are realistic. Even if once realistic, they may not be over time, as another Australian social worker explained:

> As a worker you have to meet the targets, like 'x' amount of clients per year and you've got a set amount of funding as well. The biggest problem with funding, funding hasn't changed for the last five years and the problem is they take out money for wages and office equipment things like that so it gets a little bit less for the clients, which is a shame. I think management need to fight for more money, speak to the funding bodies and say 'It's been on this level for five years and it needs to be increased'.

For some organizations, the perceived lack of congruence between the values and practices of their organization and those of government make it unlikely that any government funding would be sought. As the manager of one Australian faith-based organization which is self-funded rather than relying on government contracts stated:

> It is unlikely we will be taking state or Commonwealth money. This is because of the bureaucracy involved in state and Commonwealth grant-making, because of the dynamic between faith-based organization and the state. So, never say never, but it is unlikely that we will go for funding from government agency, unless there is a pot, as there is in the UK and the US, to fund faith-based agencies.

While largely funded from its religious community and fees paid by service users, this agency did however receive some financial and other forms of assistance from other non-government organizations with which it had some affinity. Conversely, there are faith-based organizations who may accept funds from organizations with which they have little affinity but to which they believe they have an entitlement. This includes Jewish organizations internationally which are receiving funds as a form of compensation after the Holocaust. An observation from a social worker working in a Jewish organization in Australia was that:

> One of the things that drives some of the funding at [organization] is reparation funding from the German government and other governments who provide funding through New York to all the Jewish people who live in other countries to support them because of the Holocaust.

The ambivalence of faith-based organizations towards some sources of funding is often matched by an ambivalence of funders towards faith-based organizations. A dark side may make it difficult for donors to engage with some faith-based organizations (Jennings and Clarke 2008), and while the following comments have been made in respect of the funding of international aid and development efforts, they may equally apply to domestic social welfare programmes:

> Western official donors . . . have traditionally been ambivalent about the relationship between faith and development and the activities of faith-based organizations (FBOs). Heavily influenced by the legal separation of Church and state in liberal democracies, they felt that religion was counter-developmental, that religious discourses with strong historical resonance were inflexible and unyielding in the face of social and political change. Reason and faith were constructed as oppositional, mutually incompatible spheres.
>
> (Clarke and Jennings 2008: 1)

Hence, some donors are more likely to fund programmes which they perceive to be secular, in which there is a clear distinction between welfare provision or community development and specifically religious functions of the organization (Clarke and Jennings 2008). On the other hand, there may well be funders of a strong religious persuasion who would not fund faith-based organizations which they perceive as having become too secular.

Many faith-based organizations and funders will continue, as they do now, to need each other. However, where funders have very different agendas from the organizations they fund, fulfilling the expectations of both sides is likely to require considerable and ongoing dialogue as well as assessments as to what is realistic.

Service users

While social work literature will readily depict service users as being 'other' and whose thoughts and opinions about services don't really count

(Crisp *et al.* 2005), social welfare services provided by faith-based organizations are often perceived to be of higher quality, providing a more holistic approach tailored to individual needs (Pettersson 2011), and many service users report experiencing a 'genuine interest' in them, as well as respect (Williamson 2005; Williamson and Hodges 2006). Nevertheless, it may be important that service users are made aware that the organization from which they are receiving services has a faith basis. As a social worker working for a protestant church welfare organization said:

> Right from the first visit we tell them where we're from. There was a tendency at one time in the early days of the agency where folks would say 'we're just a small agency in [city]'. I said 'No, no, you tell folk that we are part of the [religious denomination] so if they have any issues with this they can be upfront and say at that point'.

A similar point was made by the manager of a welfare organization which was part of the Catholic Church:

> I suppose, what we do stress to people when they come to us at the beginning is that we offer a service to people from all faiths and none, so again, we get a significant number of Catholic people coming to us because we are known throughout the church, etc. But we also get people who come to us by word of mouth because . . . they have been told they will get a good service from us. From that point of view, the motivation for people coming to us is pretty varied. We do tell them that we are a Catholic agency at the point that they come to us for a service and we stress that the values that inspire and drive this agency are Catholic values.

An upfront approach may occasionally result in staff providing information or making referrals to other services. However, for those who ultimately do become service users, some of the other benefits of involvement with a faith-based organization may include receiving additional services beyond what a programme is mandated to provide. When discussing the non-faith-based providers of similar services, some research participants commented on their ability to be more flexible with service users; for example:

> I think they're a little bit more black and white, we sort of fill in the grey spots. We're a lot more responsive and we can help straight away whereas they're very black and white and they get things written down for the client and that's all they'll help them with. We expand that.

Service users may also have an expectation of faith-based organizations being more responsive to their needs than other organizations and voice this to the social workers and other agency staff. For one of the social workers interviewed for this book, this meant 'I can certainly say that for some clients who don't get what they want, they're reminded that you're supposed to be God-based and you should do things because God wants you to. I'm not sure what they say to the non-secular – to the non-faith-based ones.'

A recent survey of parents of children attending faith-based day-care programmes in the US revealed that almost all respondents believed that people who were devoted to their faith were more effective human service workers, and the majority of parents had a preference for services to be staffed by people who were religious. However, it should be noted that overall ratings of staff competence were high (Edwards 2013); the question remains as to whether staff who were religious but not competent would have been preferred to highly competent staff who declared no religious affiliation.

Faith-based organizations which have accrued financial capital may not only be more flexible in what services were provided, but also in respect of reducing or waiving any fees should these apply for a service (Clark 1995). A further benefit of contact with a faith-based organization may be increased social capital (Schneider 1999), and in particular feeling a greater sense of community (Yancey and Atkinson 2004). As a social worker in a faith-based organization that works with people who have long-term mental health issues explained, most other services assumed that recovery was a realistic aim, but for those for whom this was not likely, developing a sense of community was essential:

> it is more of a community, and a lot of the people who've been involved in [organization] have been here for years, there's no trying to move them on to other, I mean, it's great, and the thing is, of course, I can understand how it's great to link people in to mainstream stuff in the community that's not psych, but the reality is there's a certain cohort of people, and for lack of a better word, the people who we mainly deal with are the longer term, more chronic presentations. And really, realistically, they have the right to have a place to be in their own community, and that's kind of what [organization] provides, where it's a very supportive community, they all look out for each other. If anyone's missing, they say, 'Where are they?' 'Are they in hospital?' If anyone's in hospital, whether it be physical issues, or mental health issues, people will go and visit them, but it really is a community of people here who look out for each other, and it's a beautiful thing, really.

Positive experiences can also result in positive recommendations to other potential service users. However, for some people, the need for a recommendation from other service users will be superfluous, particularly from those with a strong preference for services with a religious orientation (Scales and Kelly 2011). Nevertheless, while the desirability of a faith-based organization for some service users will be its ability to provide access to religious services or be sensitive to the religious needs of service users, there may be others who choose faith-based organizations if they provide services that are culturally familiar (Valins 2011).

On the other hand, there may be religious people who would be reluctant to have any contact with a welfare agency associated with their religious community for fear of having their issues becoming widely known and subject to gossip but may be open to receiving services from a provider associated with another religious tradition (Fokas 2006). Furthermore, it must be recognized that some service users will only use faith-based services when there are no other suitable services available to them. Although not necessarily a frequent occurrence, social workers in both Australia and Scotland reported the occasional service user who declined services upon learning they were to be provided by an organization with a faith base. As one explained:

> I think we still, every now and again we'll get people who will ring up and say, once they find out we're a [religious denomination] organization they don't want to come. . . . And we get some people who say, 'Oh, does that mean we're going to be forced, is there going to be religion forced down our throats?' or, 'Does that mean we're going to be told we have to stay with our partner even when we don't want to?' or does that mean 'you won't accept gay people?' or, so we still get those sorts of questions.

Same-sex couple Rose Mann and Philomena Horsley (2012) have written about their experiences with a faith-based palliative care unit while caring for Rose's brother. Expecting discrimination based on previous experiences, they were nervous about engaging with a faith-based organization and surprised not only that their fears were not realized but also by the high level of support they received. However, when the need came for further care and Rose's brother was moved to another faith-based provider, their original expectations were fulfilled:

> It had literature in the waiting room that disrespected gay relationships. Once again you feel exposed, devalued. It reinforced how important it is for all services to be upfront about recognizing and respecting lesbian and gay people, especially at times of crisis and death.
>
> (Mann and Horsley 2012)

For service users, what ultimately may be of most importance is not whether or not a service is provided by a faith-based organization, but whether the service provider will enable their needs, religious or otherwise, to be met (Fouka *et al.* 2012). When faith-based organizations decide to cease providing what service users regard as highly desirable or essential services, their appeal can greatly diminish (Jawad 2009).

Wider community

In many countries there are community-wide expectations that religious communities will be involved in welfare provision. As Michael Challen, an Anglican bishop from Australia and former head of a large welfare agency, commented:

> The people of Australia expect the Churches to be active in the care of people, whether they are members or not. This expectation has been formed, not only by the Churches delivering ministries of care over the centuries, but also by the imperatives contained within the teachings of the Christian tradition.
>
> (Challen 1996: 26)

As the wider community has expectations of faith-based organizations, so, too, faith-based organizations frequently rely on the goodwill and support of the wider community beyond. Readers may recall the case study in Chapter 2 concerning the Brotherhood of St Laurence which was widely respected not only for its service delivery, but also for shaping social policy in Australia. That a faith-based organization was so well respected in the wider community was commented on by a social worker from another faith-based organization:

> If you look at the Brotherhood of St Laurence, and the impact it has in shaping the social policy. Now obviously that's strategic as well, in terms of you know, who's in the roles. I think that even though we're a secular country, we respect religion, and so organizations that are embedded in religion have got that respect, it fits well with their ethos.

Another organization which commands wide respect internationally for its welfare services is the Salvation Army. As a social worker employed by the Salvation Army reflected:

> I think the Salvation Army specifically has a very, very good reputation in the public in general and a lot of the money that they raise is because of what they've done in the past, so the war, being out there helping the soldiers. People often talk about that. But it's also, I think, about meeting those people who are most in need. The Salvation Army . . . in

general would work with the most disadvantaged, the ones who perhaps have fallen through the system for other reasons.

Yet wide recognition doesn't necessarily equate with a good understanding of organizations such as the Salvation Army. The author has been told about social workers who had come to work for the Salvation Army and were shocked to discover that they were working for a faith-based organization. Conversely, there are others in the community who assume that all Salvation Army staff have religious roles, even though many of its welfare staff are employed on a secular basis and do not necessarily hold religious beliefs consistent with Christianity, let alone the Salvation Army. For social workers employed by the Salvation Army, this confusion in the community becomes an everyday issue to be managed:

> They do have a lot of things they are involved in and are spread widely around the community. But there is an aspect, if you are part of the Salvation Army you belong. There is a language and people perceive you as a Salvation Army officer. I wear my name tag and I get approached by people in the community all the time, coming straight up to me and there is that perception. . . . So when I go out I usually take my name badge off.

Community recognition can also facilitate donations of time and other resources from the wider community, as well as the recruitment of volunteers from beyond the religious community.

Board of management

Research on human service organizations in general has tended to pay relatively little attention to boards of management compared to other stakeholders (Ozanne and Rose 2013). This is despite the fact that any tensions among groups of stakeholders are most likely to be evidenced in the working of the board of management or legal entity which is able to employ staff and enter into contractual agreements with funding organizations. In some faith-based organizations, the faith basis is perhaps most evident at the board level, particularly if the members of the board have all been appointed by the auspicing religious community (or communities) (Schneider 1999; Vanderwoerd 2004). In some instances considerable power may reside in the hands of a nominated official in the religious hierarchy (Gardner 2006), as described by a research participant discussing the role of the most senior member of the religious hierarchy in the region:

> Well he's got full control. Sorry, he appoints the members of the incor-porated body and so he's got control there and those members become

the board. In effect they elect themselves to be on the board . . . but he has three reserve powers. To change our constitution you need a special motion, to close the agency you need a special motion of the board and to sack the director you need a special motion of the board. And to get a special motion, you need 70 per cent of the total vote and in a special motion he has 40, so you couldn't do anything if he didn't agree on those three things. The constitution keeps us tied to the church in a sense, you know, the mission. So to change the mission we can't really do it unless he wants to.

Although this situation had not necessarily been problematic in the experience of the speaker, the assumption that religious officials alone are best placed to make decisions about faith-based welfare organizations doesn't necessarily tally with the situation where board members have a fiduciary responsibility to safeguard the finances of the organization (Holden and Trembath 2008). Hence the boards of some faith-based organizations may go beyond their membership and seek to recruit community members who have particular skills which the board requires as well as the ability to commit their time to the organization (Harris *et al.* 2003). One of the Australian participants spoke of the composition of a board of management of which she was a member in which not all the board members were from the faith community:

> On the board I'm currently on we're required to have at least a third faith-based members on the board and it's really interesting to me to witness those not of the faith and the contribution that they're prepared to make to a faith-based agency, even though they don't have that faith or no faith at all, but genuinely support the work that the agency is trying to do.

Nevertheless, as this speaker went on to acknowledge, being supportive of the agency did not necessarily translate into an understanding of how the broader religious community worked. But even board members who are members of the faith community may fail to agree as to whether a faith-based welfare organization is 'a "part" of the Church, an "arm" or "instrument" of the Church' (Komonchak 1997: 38) if they don't understand the original vision. As other research participants commented, one of the key roles of the board was to maintain the overall vision for the organization which can easily be lost in responding to the needs of particular groups of stakeholders:

> it's more about them keeping us honest and keeping this back to the original focus of the agency because even though we're not particularly faith based now it was the faith that originally got us going and

they had their purpose and I guess for me having them there is a matter about bringing us back to the basics and reminding us what we're there for because quite often you get carried away. You go off on your own agenda and you do everything that the government wants you to do and the clients are wanting all this and whatnot and then you actually forget why the agency started in the first place.

In organizations which have a highly professionalized staff, the role of board members may be less hands-on management and much more focused on strategic planning and decision-making (Ebaugh *et al.* 2005). This can involve both establishing new areas of work and making decisions to withdraw from areas of work:

I'm actually on the board of an agency now . . . and we try to do strategic planning because for me faith-based agencies have always been on the edge for the most disadvantaged where government services aren't providing support and I think what's occurred over time is that we've often continued with those services beyond when they are on the edge and they've become universal services, but because of the history of the service provision, the faith-based agencies continue to be providing those services.

Being able to think strategically in changing circumstances may require a board of management to have a good grasp both of the local circumstances but also at the regional or national level, as stakeholders working at a regional or national level may have different perspectives from those working in a local area (Angell and Wyller 2006; Angell 2010).

Conclusion

As this chapter has sought to demonstrate, there can be a wide range of stakeholders in faith-based organizations, each with its own perspectives and needs (Dinham 2009), and some of whom haven't necessarily thought about the role of faith-based organizations as providers of welfare services (Angell and Wyller 2006). There may also be role blurring and stakeholders cannot necessarily be categorized into distinct groups (Netting *et al.* 2005). Balancing diverse requirements is often difficult, if not impossible, but failure to recognize the legitimate interests of some stakeholders ultimately may not make things easier for faith-based organizations. Chapter 5 will further consider the perspective of one key group, i.e. professional social work staff, and explore their experiences of working for faith-based organizations.

5
WORKING IN FAITH-BASED ORGANIZATIONS

[I]t is clearly apparent that our workforce – who can increasingly make choices about who they work for – do not come to work for Catholic agencies for better terms and conditions! In our welfare agencies in particular, workers are often asked to work for significantly lower wages than they could attract for similar roles in the public service. Our workers are often working in physical environments that are of a lower standard than other workplaces: converted school buildings, convents and houses. Yet still they come to work for us. There is little doubt that the values our agencies seek to embody form part of our attraction to these workers.

(Quinlan 2008: 51)

Introduction

The working conditions and/or the expectations placed on employees in faith-based organizations can be challenging or perceived as unreasonable by some social workers. Yet, as Quinlan has observed, faith-based organizations are clearly an attractive employment proposition for many social workers and not just those with strong religious beliefs or convictions. This chapter explores social work employment in faith-based organizations, beginning with the decision to seek work in a faith-based organization and appointment processes, and then considering working conditions and issues of career progression within faith-based organizations.

Seeking employment in a faith-based organization

There is a range of reasons why social workers seek employment in faith-based organizations which can be grouped in respect of the social worker's sense of vocation, the characteristics of the organization, and pragmatic factors. Each will be discussed in turn.

Vocation

Consistent with research findings indicating that British social workers employed by faith-based organizations were three times as likely to believe in God (Ashford and Timms 1990), working in a faith-based organization for some social workers is living out their vocation or calling (Chamiec-Case and Sherr 2006; Ebear *et al.* 2008; Schuiringa 2007). This may either be the outcome of a process of discerning what they believe is an appropriate response to a direct invitation from a deity or believing they have a particular 'calling' to offer their lives in religious service (Eastham 2002; Thyer 2006) and may have underpinned their initial decision to become a social worker. This applied to a number of research participants from both Australia and Scotland, one of whom articulated this by saying:

> I guess I originally went into social work partly because of my faith and my upbringing. So for me it's always being connected and as a member of the [religious denomination], it still really interests me what the role of the church is as far as its mission and its agency work.

Similarly in the words of another research participant:

> I personally never had an issue, because I worked out, after doing social work and having to question my own faith foundation when I did social work, that working in social work for the [faith-based organization] or whoever, for me, is about living out my Christian faith. So it's not so that I'm a Bible-basher or whatever, it's just that's how I live.

When working in secular organizations, social workers with strongly held religious beliefs may perceive that they are discriminated against due to their religion, with colleagues presuming to know how a religious person might act in a particular set of circumstances (Ressler and Hodge 2003, 2005). Seeking work in a faith-based organization may therefore be an act of self-preservation for some religiously devout social workers (Thyer and Myers 2009). As one of the Scottish social workers who worked in an organization explained:

> I also enjoy the fact that my colleagues have a Christian faith, all to a varying degree and all to, not necessarily the organization I work for, not necessarily the church I work for, which happens to be the church I go to but that is coincidental. But I enjoy the fact that, if you like, that

I can be honest about what my faith is and, but not in a forceful way that everybody has to be Christian and everybody has to believe this, that and the next thing, but the fact that it is acknowledged that I am Christian, and I like that. . . .

I was with the local authority for 14 years and for a big part of that it wasn't an issue. I don't go around shoving my faith in people's throats, I don't even tell people working, that I work for, or when I was in local authority, I didn't even tell people that I was a Christian. But latterly it had come to the point where not only were a lot of people not Christian, a lot of people were very anti-Christian and it did often make it difficult, I can think of specific occasions when following a case review I was hauled into the manager's office thinking I had done something terribly wrong and this person who was not a Christian and who was an Atheist, who actually said to me, 'Did you make these recommendations because your beliefs?', and I said, 'No', I said, 'I made the recommendations because the person that we were working with would have talked about it and would have stated that that was the recommendation that we were going to go with. It had nothing to do with my faith.'

For social workers, working with those who are the most excluded members of society is for some people the ultimate experience in religious learning not only for themselves (Warner 2009), but also in establishing a focus for their work (Ranson 2012). As another social worker explained:

I regard myself as a Christian . . . I think a lot of my motivation comes from a sort of social justice perspective where I feel I'm called to do what I can to make the world a better and fairer place, a more just place so I suppose that's where I come from as opposed to a more fundamentalist Christianity that might have a slightly different emphasis. I'm not here to proselytize or to save people or anything like that. I'm just here to do my bit to make the world a better place because of it.

A few of the Australian social workers were professional religious prior to qualifying as social workers, and who undertook their social work degrees with the expectation that this would enhance the welfare work in which they were involved. For these individuals there was typically an expectation that they would work in a faith-based welfare organization associated with their religion. As one explained:

[CEO] had put out a bit of a feeler as to whether I was interested and I wasn't because I already had other commitments and then when I

[became available] I also didn't want to go for other jobs until I had
had a courtesy conversation with [CEO] just to say 'Look I am around,
I'm looking for a job, don't need it here, but I don't want to get a job
somewhere else and then for you to hear later down the track'.

Another aspect of vocation is work which enables one to have an 'authentic
existence' (Homan 1986). This cuts across religious beliefs, such that social
workers may believe that a call to serving humanity can be realized in an
organization that is underpinned by religious beliefs very different to their
own (Ebear *et al.* 2008). As a manager of an Australian faith-based
organization which employs many staff who don't share the organization's
religious beliefs and practices suggested:

> even the people who are non-professing Christians or whoever, who
> come to work for [organization], they're not there because of God;
> they're there because they want to help people. So I think that's
> something that's really important to – that there is a sense of humanity
> in people who work in the community sector, whatever that might be
> driven by, to provide and help people who are in need.

This sense of 'calling' or 'destiny' may actually be discerned by others who
identify an individual who has the skills, values and passion for the work of
an organization (Eastham 2002). Hence, a number of the research
participants reported being invited to take up positions for which they
would not necessarily have applied. For example, a senior social worker
with management responsibilities commented: 'I was actually approached. I
was at the time working [other organization] . . . and we were going to sort
of seachange and not work so hard.' Others also noted that employment in
a faith-based organization came at a time when they were reconsidering
their life directions. As one explained:

> I was having a break . . . because I'd burned out a little . . . and that
> was when [predecessor] approached me, because he knew I was
> between jobs. . . . And then [predecessor] sort of struck at that time,
> and said 'Take over, I want to retire!' It was my relationship with
> [predecessor], and my relationship with the people, the participants in
> the programme. Because for years, probably four or five years before I
> took on the coordinator role, I'd built up a relationship with lots of the
> participants here.

Third parties may also play a role, letting social workers know of positions
which they might want to consider applying for. For example,

> someone told me of a job being advertised there . . . and I do have a
> faith, so it seemed like it was the time I was looking for work, and

I'd just done some more training in mental health, and it seemed it was all meant to be. I fell into it really, it was offered at the right time, I'd done some training, felt it suited my requirements and went for the interview.

For another social worker, the suggestion that she apply came in the form of an anonymous note from a colleague in the non-faith-based organization she was working in:

I came into the office one day and one of my colleagues, I still to this day don't know who, had left a job prospectus on my desk which they had picked up, had seen in the newspaper and had photo-copied it for me and it just said, the wee post-it on it saying, 'This is your job'.

A few research participants were approached by faith-based organizations despite being known to have religious beliefs which were very different to the organization's, or having no religious beliefs or affiliation. Such approaches often came as a surprise and were often based on having specific skills or knowledge required by an organization at the time. Hence accepting employment may be consistent with a professional but not a religious vocation. As is discussed later in this chapter, when social workers cease their employment in one faith-based organization for employment elsewhere, this does not have to be inconsistent with a sense of vocation. A vocation is not necessarily long term, but nevertheless is quite real at the time. In a published history of a prominent Australian faith-based organization, it was suggested that 'like those in an earlier religious vocation, some staff found the commitment, given and expected, left no room for anything else, including personal relationships' (Holden and Trembath 2008: 222).

Having a vocation doesn't necessarily mean that it can be realized. As mentioned previously, faith-based welfare initiatives may be limited to specific fields of practice, and there may be no suitable social work position in a faith-based organization which meets a professional's skills and expertise and other job requirements such as location. One of the research participants recalled the frustration of hearing of opportunities in a faith-based organization which resonated with her skills and values but which she felt unable to apply for, as a close relative held a senior position in the organization.

Organization characteristics

Whether or not one considers a calling to work, social workers are often keen to work in organizations in which they sense a fit with their own values. For those who seek intentionally to work in faith-based organizations, this may be in response to religious beliefs which were congruent with the agency's stance. For example,

> One of the things that attracted me . . . was their mission statement and their vision statement. So when I saw [biblical verse] . . . across the top of their literature . . . I thought well, this is an interesting organization. So this is still kind of the front across all of their literature and across their strategic plan. So I wanted to interview them really, find out why is that there and what are you on about.

For others, the sense of fit may be due to having a vision of being involved in work which aligns with professional values (Frisina 2006). Despite claiming no religious affiliation, an Australian social worker who had worked with a number of faith-based organizations remarked:

> I think there is for me personally there's something about faith-based organizations that they actually are values driven so they're driven by wanting – they're different to my experience of the private and the state government sector and I quite like that about them . . . I think it probably is their values that they're driven by are more than bureaucracy or money that there's something core to what they do and I think that gives them a lot of strength. And certainly I'm attracted to work for those sorts of organizations because of that.

Being 'struck by the integrity of the staff that worked there' was the experience of another research participant who had applied for a position in an agency with which she was in contact in her role in another agency. She went on to say:

> I think there was just a bit of a layer I suppose of caring that wasn't always present in some other agencies. It's hard to define what exactly that was, but it was something to do with the depth of caring that went just beyond the immediate role that staff were playing. Hard to define really because not all the staff were Christian necessarily, certainly not [religious denomination], but just a commitment to clients I think.

Whereas for the previous speaker there was a high degree of congruence between her own religious beliefs and the agency's practices, the value basis of an agency may also find resonance among social workers who do not regard themselves as being religious, or having any knowledge of or interest in religion. For example, as one social worker recalled,

> I remember when I did my bachelor that I was there going 'I'm not going to work in a faith-based agency' . . . I was like 'Oh I'm not going

to work in there. They'll want me to be Catholic or they'll want me to be Christian or they'll have lots and lots of rules because it's a church' and stuff. Whereas having worked at heaps of them I've realized that that's actually the best place for me and I'm not religious at all. I have never read the Bible, don't know anything about any of them. So sometimes I have people come up with stuff and I'm like 'I have no idea what you're talking about' but in some ways that actually works to my benefit as well. It means that I don't have any of my own values that I'm placing on them because of my own religion.

Some wariness is nevertheless warranted by social workers, irrespective of their religious beliefs, and they will avoid employment in organizations where they do not feel comfortable with the prevailing values (Gardner 2011). Whereas social work training in many countries stresses anti-oppressive practice approaches along with structural and feminist analyses and a commitment to social justice, the experiences of social work students and new graduates in some faith-based organizations is that such ways of working mean that sometimes principles are 'often dismissed, ignored or actively opposed' (Larson and Robertson 2007: 252).

Pragmatic reasons

The need to gain employment rather than a sense of vocation or desire to work in a specific agency was particularly evident among some of the Australian research participants who commenced work in faith-based organizations as newly qualified social work graduates. Whereas for a few, final placements as part of their social work degree led to the offer of employment, for others it was just a matter of chance that they were offered employment in a faith-based organization which they had applied for on pragmatic grounds. As one early career social worker recalled:

> I'm quite interested in the mental health side, but it was also as an acknowledgement that as a new graduate with only the Bachelor's degree under my belt, I couldn't be too picky with where I went, so I applied for a lot of different jobs.

But what may start as just getting a job can turn into a long-term career prospect. Another social worker, having initially obtained short-term employment on graduation several years prior to interview, nevertheless found the agency ethos to his liking, saying, 'I like the way they help their clients, it's very client-focused and client-centred which is good and it's in line with social work'.

It is not just new graduates but also experienced social workers who at times find themselves in need of employment and needing to take positions which they might in other circumstances avoid. Some participants had taken on locum (short-term) positions because they needed paid work but later came to embrace organizations which in the words of one research participant were based on a culture and traditions which were 'very foreign' to anything she had previously experienced. Another participant who took up a short-term position at a difficult time in her life reflected:

> I was working at [previous organization] which is another faith-based organization, and I was made redundant, and so I was just looking for anything really. The [current organization] job was advertised, and the one I took was a locum position as a case manager in a residential facility. I thought, OK, locum is good. I don't really know what I'm doing. I had a few personal issues at the time and I thought that's a really good way to just settle, and then I just found I liked [current organization] . . . I didn't know that I was going to love that, but I found it, yeah, just a really nice place to be.

While the previous speaker initially took a position because she needed to gain employment, two other research participants sought positions in faith-based organizations due to the fact that their domestic lives were incompatible with their previous positions as a result of travel time or the hours of work. When job opportunities which used their expertise and were compatible with their domestic situations emerged, they applied for such positions, with employment in a faith-based organization being serendipitous. Interestingly, pragmatic factors were not uncommon in Clark's (1995) sample of workers in an Islamic clinic in Egypt.

While recognizing that some social workers may seek positions for essentially pragmatic reasons, there may nevertheless be held a hope that a deeper commitment to the work of the organization might evolve, as expressed in the following words by a senior member of staff in a large Australian faith-based organization:

> I think there are other people who come to work here just because it's another social work job and it offers a good place to work and the conditions are good and whatever. I think people's motivations are different but I guess that, probably my hope would be . . . the organization that could influence the people who come to work here. So it would add an extra dimension to you as a worker, and somehow that would add an extra dimension in terms of striving to do the best service you could for the people.

Appointment processes

Individual social workers putting themselves forward or allowing their name to be put forward for a position is only one side of the employment equation. What is equally important is consideration as to how faith-based organizations appoint and induct new staff into the workplace.

Staff selection

Some understandings of faith-based organizations assume that all staff will be persons of the faith (Thyer 2006). For example, Crossreach, the welfare agency of the Church of Scotland, has gained approval to make it an occupational requirement that all staff working directly with service users be Christians (Crossreach 2013b). One rationale for such a stance is an underlying belief that workers with a strong faith are more attuned to the needs of service users than are non-believers (Cnaan and Boddie 2006). In such organizations, religious beliefs are not just a requirement for appointment but also for promotion, and staff may be expected to participate in religious activities within the organization (Lake 2013). While there are undoubtedly many faith-based organizations which insist on employing persons of faith providing exemplary services, if professional competence is considered to be less important in staff selection than religious faith, this may lead to 'a culture defined more by parochialism than clinical excellence' (Lake 2013: 173).

In his first encyclical, *Deus Caritas Est*, the former Pope Benedict XVI indicated what he regards as the standards of staff employed in Catholic welfare agencies:

> Individuals who care for those in need must first be professionally competent: they should be properly trained in what to do and how to do it, and committed to continuing care. Yet, while professional competence is a primary, fundamental requirement, it is not of itself sufficient. We are dealing with human beings, and human beings always need something more than technically proper care. They need humanity. They need heartfelt concern. Those who work for the Church's charitable organizations must be distinguished by the fact that they do not merely meet the needs of the moment, but they dedicate themselves to others with heartfelt concern, enabling them to experience the richness of their humanity. Consequently, in addition to their necessary professional training, these charity workers need a 'formation of the heart': they need to be led to that encounter with God in Christ which awakens their love and opens their spirits to others.
>
> (Benedict XVI 2006: section 31a)

This ideal of staff who are both professionally competent and whose religious beliefs are consistent with the organization is however something which many faith-based welfare agencies struggle to realize. Many agencies which may historically have insisted upon staff being of their religion no longer have this requirement and staff selection processes may have 'developed in such a way that the professional integrity of the people was probably paramount rather than their . . . beliefs'. As a former manager of a large Australian faith-based organization observed, 'in the end . . . there's not so many social workers out there, and there's even less who may be professing Christians. That's a generalised statement. But yeah, I think it causes them some issues, yeah. Certainly some of the hierarchy.'

Not only are there staff who do not share the religious leanings of the employing organization but in many agencies a wide mix of religions is represented among the staff. The following description is far from atypical in faith-based welfare organizations in Australia:

> I think it's got a broader focus and it's much less [Christian denomination] focused than it was, that's changed, a broader understanding of people. We have a staff gathering now and you've got Jewish people, you've got Muslim people, you've got Buddhists, we've got a diversity of nationalities and religions on the staff.

This requires an acceptance of diversity from both the organization and individual staff, and limits expectations that staff will participate in religious activities that are aligned with the organization or its ethos (cf. Larson and Robertson 2007). As an Australian social worker in a different agency commented, 'I come from the Buddhist faith, but I work in a Christian organization, and I've got no issues, either way, and just acknowledge that it's a different teaching, and it's a different religion, but the biggest thing is that there is acceptance from each side'.

Conversely, there is no guaranteed fit even for social workers who come from the same religious tradition as the organization. A social worker in an agency which provided services for Jewish clients commented that 'there are many shades of grey in being Jewish . . . there are secular Jews right through to sort of Orthodox Jews'. And as one Christian reflected, 'I don't think you need to be a Christian to work in a faith-based organization. In my experience, you'll probably get more frustrated in a faith-based organization, or Christian-based organization, if you are.'

This reflects that there may be many ways in which religious beliefs can be operationalized by an organization and, even in apparently similar organizations, the form and extent of explicit expressions of religious beliefs vary considerably in the service delivery context (Larson and Robertson 2007). Whereas for one research participant part of the fit between herself and her place of employment was that the organization saw its role as 'service' and not 'mission', one might expect frustrations when expectations of the agency role are unmet.

Although it is recognized that not all staff will share the same religious beliefs or outlook, there may be expectations of a fit with the organization's value base (Conradson 2011; Rogers 2009). As one senior manager commented, 'We hire broadly. The issue around hiring is "are you committed to our mission and our values?" If not then it's best for you to go.' This fit of values is typically tested in job interviews, and explicit discussion of religious beliefs and values is a factor that often distinguishes the employ-ment process in faith-based organizations from other welfare agencies (Conradson 2011). In large organizations, the responsibility for testing this may lie with the chief executive officer or a small number of senior staff recognized as having a well-developed understanding of the organizational ethos. As a senior staff member in a large organization reflected, this was accepted practice within the agency even by staff who did not feel comfortable asking such questions themselves:

> Sometimes when you would go to be on an interview panel with people and you would be dividing up the questions and someone would go, '[name], can you ask that faith one at the end, we don't know how to ask that but you will'. Whereas in a way for me that is a really important question, coming into the organization, that people can respect the values that we stand for.

Nevertheless, this social worker recalled that when she graduated as a social worker more than 30 year earlier, the potential for questions of faith to be included in a job interview was a deterrent to applying for a position in a faith-based organization:

> When I first started to work, and I can remember listening to people who were working in organizations that had a connection to the Church, and I remember the word, that there was great anxiety about how you would answer the question if you were asked, if you were going to work for one of the then Anglican agencies. I can remember people saying well this is how you would answer the question if you were asked this, so I think if anything, at the time I would have been graduating, there would have been a powerful pull to absolutely separate any faith connection with your place of work.

In some jurisdictions, religious organizations, including the welfare agencies under their auspice, are exempted from some provisions around discrimination in employment law (Cnaan *et al.* 1999). Such provisions have been used to justify not hiring on the basis of factors including their sexuality, lifestyles and religious beliefs and practices if inconsistent with the values and belief basis of the organization (Cnaan *et al.* 1999; Ebear *et al.* 2008). While there are some faith-based organizations which require staff to sign a statement of faith (Thaut 2009), many faith-based organizations take a more pragmatic stance, employing a wide range of staff providing that they can accept the mission statement or other similar documents (Vanderwoerd 2004). Prospective employees may be asked to comment on the content of such documents at interview. As the manager of an Australian faith-based organization explained:

> [P]eople are asked when we interview them, we always give them a mission statement and the values and so on, and say, 'Why have you applied to ?' . . . So they don't have to sign the dotted line and say they're going to church three times a month or whatever, but we do, they do need to feel like there is a fit between their own personal lifestyle and their own personal framework and how they view life, and the way that we work.

This was certainly the experience of some Australian social workers when being interviewed by a faith-based organization and who were not religious or of another faith:

> When we are interviewed, we are told that you don't have to be religious, that's not forced upon you but the underpinnings of our work are done to the ethics and principles of the [religion] which we work by. So they've got their own code of ethics which we have to follow. Do they force religion on us, no not at all. I think you have to be, just like in any other agency, go with their underpinnings of what they see as their work and stick up for their reputation when you are working in the community.

Yet for social workers who were not religious or who held beliefs which were different from the agency in which they were seeking employment, the interview process was not necessarily straightforward. As one explained:

> It actually made me hesitate, because I'm not a Christian, and then I had to be very careful with the philosophy that the [organization] has, and it was actually asked of me in the interview, something about, and I can't for the life of me remember the answer that I gave, but I did acknowledge right from the very start that my issue was going to be that the [organization] requests that people try and make disciples.

Despite the responses given at interview, this social worker was offered a position in the agency, suggesting that in practice the agency was more flexible with some aspects of its protocol than might be envisaged from a reading of documentation issued with a job description to potential employees.

Staff induction

Apart from questions at interview ascertaining fit with an organization's religious ethos, one of the times when the religious origins of a welfare organization are most likely to be discussed explicitly is during the induction of new staff. Although there are some faith-based organizations which do not consider their origins to be of much relevance to current staff, telling how the work emerged is a common characteristic. One way of maintaining a religious identity is to ensure that new staff and board members are taught the stories of the founders and of the religious tradition (Sinha 2013). Such individuals are frequently regarded as inspirational, and not just to members of a particular religious faith or community. As a senior manager who often participated in induction events reflected:

> I think people that come to work here, we have a mix of people from those who profess to be Christians to those who aren't and people who don't really care. But most of them can connect with the stories somehow and connect with the values that underpin those, the values of the founders. It's something that we hold quite dear in the organization.

Recalling her own induction to a large faith-based organization, an Australian social worker who did not regard herself as being religious commented:

> Orientations are typically a really, really boring day. Really, really boring policies, procedures and everything like that whereas the [organization] one was fantastic where they actually explained how each part of it started and why it started and who the people were and what and that they were around during the feminist wave and all this stuff and how that had impacted and how it was during the depression that these things had started and that the different ministers had got together and said 'We need to help each other' and stuff and so that reminded you of why you were doing social work and why you were here.

In Roman Catholic agencies, particularly those run by religious orders, the prominent founders were not necessarily the individuals who established the current welfare agency but the founders of the religious orders, who may have been alive hundreds of years ago or when the order came to work in this place. As an Australian social worker commented, 'when I worked for [Catholic organization] we were all taught about the sisters and . . . how they came over from Ireland'. Although this would have occurred in the latter part of the nineteenth or early part of the twentieth century, their story was still inspiring for a twenty-first-century non-Catholic social worker. Not all faith-based organizations place such importance on the stories of their founders, such that even social workers who have previous experiences of working in a faith-based organization could find it 'amazing, that here was this organization that was so connected to its history and it's values that it had a position there to maintain that'.

As well as connecting with the past vision, many faith-based organizations also consider it important that staff connect in some way with the wider faith community associated with welfare provision. One way in which this may occur involves having religious professionals or other board members who represent the wider religious community meet with new staff.

Working as a social worker

Given that faith-based organizations may adopt distinctive practices in the recruitment and induction of new staff, it follows that experiences of practising social work in faith-based organizations may also be distinctive. This will include exploring the nature of social work practice, the scope for religious expression in the workplace, the organizational culture, the physical environment and remuneration.

The nature of social work practice

The opportunity to practise in ways which are in accord with one's vision of what professional social work should be (Collins 2008) was a recurring theme in the interviews with social workers. An important aspect of this is being client-centred which one social worker who had previously worked in a statutory child protection service noted, the faith-based organization where she now works seeks to provide the service which clients need rather than delivering a formulaic approach to the work. Furthermore, she noted the degree of professional autonomy she was accorded provided her proposals were cost-effective:

> Well the reason I left child protection, I wasn't there for long I only stayed a few months, because I went in there with the vision that I guess the child is your first client, your primary client, but your aim is to get the families back together. That is your aim. Whereas every time I'd say 'I want to do this with the family. I want to do this with the family or whatever.' They'd say 'No, no. No, no. That's not your job. That's not your job. If they want their kid back they'll do it themselves' and I was like 'Well they have to know what's there'. But they were continually putting up walls that I wasn't allowed to do all these things and so then when I went to the not-for-profits I'd come up with these ideas and they're like 'Go ahead. Go ahead. If it's not going to cost us

money then go ahead.' Obviously they never had as much money as everybody else so as long as you say that it's not going to cost them any more money and that you're still going to do your normal job then they're happy for that and I think out of all of them [organization] has been the best one with those. They actually listen to what the staff have to say and will take it on board and for instance they've let me create a [new programme] and they're more than happy. I've got all these people putting their hands up to help me and to work on it and everything else whereas everywhere else has just been like 'Oh no we don't have time to do that. There's someone in head office who'll do that' or something. So they're really keen to let people do what they think as long as you can say it's going to benefit the clients and it's not going to cost too much money.

Hence, it is not necessarily the faith basis that makes an agency attractive to some of its professional workforce but rather its ability to enable them to work with professional integrity and to provide the best possible services for disadvantaged and marginalized members of the community. However, the growing imposition of a compliance culture places small faith-based and other non-government organizations at risk of becoming acolytes of the bureaucracies. External funding frequently brings reporting demands which justify how funds have been spent and for small amounts of money in particular; the efforts to demonstrate compliance may be quite disproportionate to the efforts expended in service delivery. This is invariably reflected in the work of social workers. Discussing the growing compliance demands, an agency manager commented, 'You do wonder whether it has gone overboard. So where the balance is we will come to realize. I don't know. . . . And it could become very dominant, so it depends very much on how the management and the leadership of the organization manage that.'

Religious expression

One issue around which organizations may have clear protocols concerns religious expression. These can cover factors including dietary guidelines which concur with religious teaching, observance of religious holidays, the presence of religious symbols in the workplace, as well as guidance on 'sharing one's faith', including guidelines as to whether or not it is appropriate for workers to pray for clients (Schuiringa 2007). Even if it is not required of them, staff may feel a sense of permission to engage in conversations around matters of religion or spirituality which is often lacking in secular organizations (Gardner 2011; Gilligan 2009) even if not initiating such conversations themselves. In some faith-based organizations, service users will from time to time request that a social worker prays for them or even with them, and this request may be granted. For example, the experience of some social workers is that:

> People might have things they want to discuss about spirituality and other things, and they know that they can target me, or some of the other volunteers . . . so they know that stuff's available, but it's not very down your throat, by any stretch of the imagination.

Within other organizations service users may receive a variety of responses, depending on to whom they make such a request, and how comfortable or uncomfortable the recipient is with the request:

> It's interesting that sometimes I will be working with people and they will say to me 'Will you pray for me?' because they are going to have an operation or something like that. Now [name], my colleague who works here with me gets asked that question, she would have to say 'No' she can't pray because she doesn't believe in that but sometimes she has been known to say 'No, but I'll give it to [name]'.

Social workers who hold religious beliefs may distinguish between praying *with* service users and praying *for* them (Chamiec-Case and Sherr 2006), believing that praying for a service user is more appropriate than praying with them. However, there are others who, despite their own religious beliefs, would even consider praying for a client to be an appropriate action for a professional social worker. For example:

> I don't consciously pray for clients but I might hold someone before God or just that thought might go through my mind subconsciously but that's not something that I would discuss with people. That's just my personal approach about being a professional.

In faith-based organizations which do not require staff to have specific religious beliefs, there may also be guidelines as to what religious observances occur in staff forums. For example, in some faith-based welfare organizations, 'there's an ambivalence about practising religion in a professional environment. For example, we never have a prayer at our manager's meeting, we have reflection which is a little less direct.' Although this may be viewed as an unacceptable compromise diluting the message, such an approach could be far more effective in engaging with staff of other religious beliefs, as was the experience of the following speaker:

> I loved the fact that we had reflection time . . . I was working in a religious organization, none of this, just ghastly stuff, and here I am in a religious organization that's not of my own religion, but I felt

incredibly connected, not to the actual faith, not to the religious side of it, but to the concept of spirituality.

Organizational culture

Faith-based organizations can be attractive places to work for a wide range of social workers, and not only for those who believe that this is a place where they can live out their beliefs. Notwithstanding that there were some research participants who had experienced difficulties, in some cases leading to leaving an employer, these were typically discussed in respect of specific organizations rather than being a generalized issue with faith-based organizations. While acknowledging that this was not always the case, having been forced out of a position in a faith-based organization associated with her own religious community, one research participant commented on the importance of feeling valued, especially by a faith-based organization associated with a very different religious tradition to her own:

> I did feel valued. I absolutely felt valued at [organization], and I don't know if that's just my good luck or the people who are there or whatever, but there's something about it. If you speak to other people they'll have a different experience, I know that, because I know there are people who feel valued, and in fact, there were people who were there at the same time as me, who I know left, feeling very burnt.

While individuals may feel valued or not in any type of organization, what typified many of the faith-based organizations which employed the research participants was an organizational culture which valued its employees and acknowledged the difficulty of the work that they do. On a day-to-day basis, the encouragement of colleagues may be crucial in maintaining a positive outlook, as one social worker explained:

> There's a great spirit amongst the staff here. They're really easy to get on with, easy to talk to. They're people I trust too. I can share things with them and know that it will be fine to talk with them, they're a trustworthy group of people. I know that they have that same sort of concern for people, the way they talk about their clients and everything is really quite exciting in what they want for the people they work for, it's a really genuine worry for people and care for them.

Notwithstanding the importance of strong collegial relationships, the role of the leadership team may be integral, not only in implementing policies and procedures which aim to facilitate a positive working environment, but also in modelling working relationships which enable employees to feel valued.

As the manager of one organization remarked, how she treated her staff was an expression of her faith (Chamiec-Case and Sherr 2006):

> And I think it is around, we do believe that there is a God beyond ourselves that is present in the work that we do. And some of us, not everybody, but I was aware that I am a channel of God's love and God's hope in the work that I do and that's the way that I intend to treat my staff, and that's the way I tend to treat my clients.

This may be much easier in small organizations in which all staff are known personally than in large welfare organizations employing hundreds of staff on multiple sites. It is ironic that while growth based on taking up new funding opportunities may make a faith-based organization economically more viable, growth may lead to significant challenges for organizations which value their staff, and place a strong emphasis on the importance of positive working relationships. This was certainly a concern for the director of one Australian faith-based organization which had grown from a very small organization with a handful of staff to now employing more than 150 staff:

> I was alluding to before when saying some of those smaller agencies that are relational, they are at risk of losing that kind of relational component but I think the leadership of the organization is very, very important around making a difference and requiring staff to be different.

In this particular organization, becoming larger necessitated a more professional infrastructure and enabled staff to focus on their areas of expertise:

> I think it is easier to have best practice and I think it is also easier to have kind of infrastructure support for your work. If you have got the right people there, there is flexibility with the money, whereas, and workers can do the job they are employed to do, whereas in some of the smaller organizations you have got one social worker also doing a range of other things – they are also responsible for the OH&S and they are also responsible for . . . you get spread too thinly.

Physical environment

As in many not-for-profit community organizations, the physical environments in which many social workers work are often a world apart from the purposely designed offices of the government departments which approve much of their funding. It is not uncommon for religious groups or organizations, particularly those which are well established, to have acquired properties which are no longer required for their initial usage, including schools, churches and residential institutions (Murray *et al.* 2009) and which they make available to welfare programmes either at no cost or below market rental (Grønbjerg and Nelson 1998). Although there are some faith-based organizations which house staff in modern offices, many of the interviews for this book in both Scotland and Australia took place in buildings which have been converted from their original purposes, including houses and residential institutions. This can result in agency settings which are much less intimidating for service users to enter. As a social worker whose office is in a converted house commented:

> We've always wanted it to be a place that when people came here they felt welcome, it's one of the reasons I like the building for one thing, I think the building helps, it's a place where people come in and they'll often comment on, it's not like going to a government office or something where there's offices with your grey walls and your blank places, they come feeling there's something about the place, it's a lovely house.

However, while houses may be comfortable venues for services users to visit, they don't necessarily make good working environments. Recognizing that her workplace was not necessarily typical for a faith-based organization, a social worker in another agency, also based in a converted house, reflected:

> I think we've been fortunate to have been provided with a very nice working environment and I think that people really appreciate that. There are some places where you work where people are stacked three or four to a room and there's all second-hand furniture.

This particular agency, where possible, in a wide range of ways seeks to invest in its staff members, whom it regards as assets which need to be well treated, which includes having appropriate spaces to work. As a large agency with a long history, unlike some other agencies it has access to some of the financial resources of its founders in addition to recurrent programme funding, which mostly funds salaries. This has enabled the renovation of buildings originally built for other purposes into congenial working spaces.

For some organizations, the acquisition of modern new workplaces has been a consequence of programme expansion. Whereas small welfare organizations with a few staff may be able to accommodate their workforce in refurbished houses or in a suite of offices within the headquarters of the religious auspice, growth beyond a certain point may result in organizations needing to seek out their own accommodation and renting or purchasing office blocks which can fundamentally change the workplace dynamic. For social workers working in converted houses, the space in which they work with service users may be their own office, but the move to an office block, especially open-plan settings, means that service users are typically seen in a meeting room away from one's desk. In some instances, this may result in an agency initially appearing to be not so different from services provided by government authorities.

Remuneration

Not one of the 20 Australian and five Scottish social workers interviewed during the research for this book indicated that the financial remuneration was one of the attractive features of their employment. This is not surprising, given that faith-based organizations often have a reputation for not offering generous levels of remuneration (Holden and Trembath 2008; Lake 2013). Many Scottish and Australian welfare agencies, which align with Torry's (2005) definition of being 'faith-based' as opposed to 'religious' organizations, pay social workers at rates similar to those paid more generally by non-government organizations, but often below those paid by the public sector. Pay rates in religious organizations may even be lower if paid as a salaried religious rather than as a social worker. However, to some extent, other factors may compensate for what some may consider inadequate financial remuneration. As one Australian social worker commented:

> I've said to people, along the ways, that you can choose to work in this field and you can work at any number of organizations, and what [organization] has to offer, is its connection to soul, and to the stories of the [founders]. And, that's what it has over and above the other ones. So everyone might have something, they all pay terribly, the work is hard, the work is stressful, and I think this is, kind of, an added dimension that I think can really make the difference for people if it's connected into.

The same social worker, who had employment experience in both faith-based organizations associated with her own religious tradition and of a religious tradition quite unlike her own, noted:

> You know, it's funny, but people talk about, 'This organization pays above award rates', and 'That organization allows you a car package', and I don't know how different organizations do it, but I guess it depends on their donor bases. But in a way, I see what faith-based organizations provide is the same thing, it's kind of a boost to your salary, and it allows you to be a more rounded – and for people who are of the faith, I guess the experience of added value is . . . about adding back to your own broader community.

Even though the level of salary may not be an incentive, for those who understand their work in terms of a religious vocation, being paid to carry out what they perceive as their calling may be considered to be a privilege. As the manager of one agency said:

> It's just a wonderful place to work. Absolutely outstanding. I'm very happy and I think my team are happy. We have a very low turnover, very low turnover. So I think there's that link to calling is very strong. I get paid for my role, but you know, I feel very strongly called to it. And I've worked for a number of different government agencies . . . but I've never been so happy working here.

As few social workers work in the private-for-profit sector, the salary differential between those employed in faith-based organizations and those employed elsewhere is much smaller than in some other occupations. As the manager of one large welfare agency commented:

> we've got some really skilled IT people who would earn a fortune out in the market if they wanted to. One of them had come from a big international company and he says it's not the money, it's more around what it's doing and what we're doing to help. We've got to pay him a fair salary but he'd be earning probably three times what we got . . . but at the moment he's happy working here because I think it's the values and the mission.

Any non-financial benefits provided by working in faith-based organizations may be lost if social workers do not feel that their contributions are valued by their employers. During 2012 when interviews were being conducted with Australian social workers, national reforms of the pay and remuneration of workers in the Social and Community Services (SACS) sector were occurring with the aim of making employment much more attractive. However, in many agencies progress on salary reform was slow, leaving workers angry, disenchanted and willing to withdraw their labour (Hingston 2012), as one of the research participants elaborated:

> I think probably a lot of it's got to do with money. I know it's all supposedly changing because they said they're going to do equal pay and that the SACS award is all getting great. They said that at the start of the year. Pays still haven't changed and if you can't pay the same amount as a hospital and everything else then you can't get the staff and so then you end up with less qualified staff and you can end up with an inferior service which doesn't do you any good.

Ultimately such situations place faith-based organizations at risk of being unable to attract the most qualified, competent and experienced staff (Holden and Trembath 2008). As salaries are a major component in the budgets of already well-stretched faith-based welfare organizations, increasing salaries may only be an option if income rises correspondingly or overall staff hours are reduced. The latter option tends to be unpalatable if service users become less able to access services, and may not be possible for funded programmes without compromising funding agreements. Hence, unless appropriate funding levels are secured, faith-based organizations to an extent will continue to gamble on staff commitment being maintained and an insufficiency of better paid positions which may entice staff to leave (Lake 2013).

Career progression

Opportunities for career progression are afforded through participation in professional development activities and/or by moving on to other places of employment. Both of these will now be discussed.

Professional development opportunities

Ideally, it has been proposed that in faith-based organizations, the working practices should reflect the religious values upon which the agency is supposedly based. This may include an expectation of just working practices, in which workers are not mistreated or overworked. They should also be places where staff can grow and develop, both in themselves and in their understanding of the meaning of their work, which in turn may require the organization to invest in its workers (Ogilvie 2008). Many of the social workers who participated in this research reported opportunities for ongoing professional development during their employment in faith-based organizations. Indeed, it would seem that many organizations realized that this was an imperative to retain staff long term.

Like most organizations which employ staff, faith-based organizations usually have a range of written policies and procedures concerning employees and their working conditions, including staff development (Yancey *et al.* 2009), with these procedures more likely to be formalized in larger organizations. As with many organizations, the limitations on staff participating in training opportunities tend to be concerned with the costs. As a social worker in a very small organization reflected:

> There are all these great things, but they cost a fortune, and they cost time, so I have to cherry-pick a bit. . . . I go to the bits and pieces that I see around, if there's anyone giving a particular talk on something, and it might be free, or it might be cheap, then I just book those in my diary, and I go in my own time. But it is tricky, yeah.

A history of limited funds to spend on training can have a continuing influence even when no longer warranted. As the manager of one programme fully funded from an external source discovered, despite being provided with the funding to send staff on training and this being a component of the funding agreement, the organization would not approve staff participating in training additional to that which they were entitled to in other programmes within the organization:

> [Funding body] tell me that I'm allowed to send my staff on training as much as I like, it's my discretion about sending staff to training. And then the [organization] releases a document which says they can only go to training five times a year and under a certain amount of funding. It's not their funding – the funding's coming through the programme, so I'm stuck in a quandary . . . If I go over that, it means my staff member can't go to any more training in that year. I just looked at it and I found it incredible. If it's possible I send staff to free training.

While much of the training in which social workers in faith-based organizations participate is similar to that of social workers in other types of organizations, a few social workers reported opportunities to gain a deeper knowledge or insights into the religious ethos of the organization. In some organizations, the rationale for this is that the staff members involved are among the leadership group involved in setting and/or maintaining strategic directions and it is therefore imperative that at least some of this group have a well-developed grasp of the agency's religious roots. Although corporate expressions of spirituality are not the same as personal ones (Chamiec-Case and Sherr 2006), it is nevertheless acknowledged that opportunities which emerge from working in a faith-based organization can provide an opportunity to explore the integration of one's own beliefs within professional social work (Larson and Robertson 2007) and may lead to a deepening of one's own religious beliefs or spiritual practices (Griffiths 2011).

Professional development may also occur through opportunities for promotion and taking up positions with greater levels of responsibility. In some faith-based welfare organizations the most senior positions are reserved for professional religious, with ordination being regarded as more critical than social work training (Holden and Trembath 2008). Such appointments can create tensions for social workers who may have different understandings as to what the work of an organization should be:

> [T]hose with positions of responsibility in religious organizations tend to be trained for their roles in theological colleges or similar, and these organizations see themselves as having a primarily theological task, with the organizations which their students will serve being regarded

as theological realities related to an underlying theological position rather than as the heart of the matter.

(Torry 2005: 5)

There are some heads of welfare agencies who have both religious and social work qualifications but many are qualified in only one of these fields. When senior managers in faith-based organizations are appointed on the basis of theological qualifications rather than being social work trained, some social workers perceived that there is a glass ceiling in respect of their career prospects. As a relatively newly qualified social worker replied to a question about her career prospects within her current place of employment:

> My opportunities are limited no further than, I think it's [senior position], although that's a pretty big job in itself, but yes, if you're [a professional religious] in the church, your career opportunities within the [organization] are significantly larger.

Where there has been a demise in the requirement for clergy to be in charge, this has also opened up opportunities for more female social workers to take on leadership roles in faith-based welfare organizations (Holden and Trembath 2008).

Ceasing employment in a faith-based organization

The career paths of social workers often involve movements from one organization to another and a career within a single organization is atypical. Many of the reasons why individual social workers choose to leave faith-based organizations are similar to the reasons why social workers more generally change their employment – new opportunities, better pay, feeling burnt out, clashes with management or colleagues, the belief that another organization may be a better fit with one's skills or values, a contract expiring with no funds available to continue the position and so on. Several of the social workers who were interviewed for this project had been employed in more than one faith-based organization, and those not currently working in the sector had not necessarily ruled out this option in the future. As one social worker said, 'I would look to go back to a faith-based agency though in the future. I haven't moved away from them because of not being happy or the issues. It's just been more opportunities, yeah.'

The research process revealed a few stories of social workers who had left positions because when first employed they had not realized that the employer had some form of religious or faith basis, which is quite surprising given that a cursory look at the webpages of the organizations in which this was reported made explicit reference to underpinning religious beliefs. What is probably more common is social workers who have gained employment in a specific organization which aligns with their religious beliefs but who over time become uncomfortable with aspects of operational practice. This could either be a general feeling of discomfort or disagreements with specific policies or procedures. For one social worker who had worked with a particular organization both prior and subsequent to qualifying as a social worker, studies which exposed them to new ways of working made it difficult to remain:

> I continued to develop and expand my own knowledge and I realized that some of the things that were occurring within the organization where I worked could have been done differently. Suggestions weren't necessarily accepted very well . . . so in the end I chose to go elsewhere.

Conversely, holding religious beliefs which align with or being a member of a religious community which auspices faith-based welfare initiatives does not ensure immunity from the possibility of losing one's position, as another research participant explained:

> I got sucked into doing the [organization] and I really became quite passionate about the concept of working within my own community, and kind of what that means, not just working for the community but working for a community that's very much, very tangibly your own . . . the new management came in, and they didn't like me, so they made my role and another person's role redundant, so I felt really burned at the end of that because I had really put my heart – I had kind of opened up my heart in a way that I hadn't expected to, and so I didn't know what to do after that really.

For social workers with strong religious beliefs and where those beliefs received prominent and explicit recognition in the workplace, severing the nexus between their beliefs and place of employment may not only lead to a career crisis but also to a religious crisis (Schuiringa 2007). After ceasing employment for a religious group with whom there had been a long personal association pre-dating employment, continuing involvement in the religious activities of this organization was not an option for one of the research participants at the time of interview. This may reflect a strong sense of vocation rather than having been in employment which was a 'good fit', as there were other participants with strong religious beliefs who had moved on to other employment and maintained connections with either the faith-based welfare organization or its religious auspice.

Having left faith-based organizations to work in other sectors, social workers may find surprising similarities once the explicitly religious artefacts are stripped away. Upon moving to a senior position in government, one research participant reflected:

> I think working in government is a whole new learning again for me, because you're working in a political environment, not just government politics but some people politics. Mind you, there's people politics in the [religion] too, but they always garnished it with 'this is what Jesus wants' or 'this is what, in the name of the Bible, what you should do'. That's said with a bit of tongue in cheek, but there's also an element in that which is true. Whereas in the government, it's not necessarily around in God's name or whatever; it's 'this will suit me better, or you better, or them better' or whatever.

Conclusion

Although working in a faith-based organization can be simply one variant of working in a non-government or non-statutory voluntary welfare organization, for many of the research participants, working in a faith-based organization is a distinctive experience. While for some this provides an opportunity to combine employment with a form of religious vocation whether formally recognized or not, frequently what is distinctive are the underlying values or organizational culture, which often reflect religious values implicitly if not explicitly. In particular, individual social workers often report feeling valued, and also that their work is valued. The extent to which explicit expressions of religion impact upon the working lives of social workers in faith-based organizations differs considerably, sometimes even within the same organization, where social workers may choose whether or not to participate in religious activities associated with the organization or respond to service users who wish to discuss matters of a religious or spiritual nature.

It is perhaps not surprising that social workers who have volunteered to participate in research about social work in faith-based organizations are mostly positive, and often passionate, about their experiences of working in this sector. Even those who were working elsewhere at the time of interview had many experiences which had made positive contributions to their professional and/or personal development. Nevertheless, faith-based organizations should not take it for granted that they will always be an attractive employment for either current or prospective staff. Chapter 6 will further consider the working experiences of social workers in faith-based organizations by focusing on ethical issues.

6

ETHICAL PRACTICE IN FAITH-BASED ORGANIZATIONS

Therefore, a religious perspective on welfare should be considered a value system on which social welfare can be pursued. As an inherently moral and ethical discourse, religious welfare merely reaffirms that all perspectives to social welfare bury within them certain ideological and normative convictions about the nature of the good society.

(Jawad 2009: 255)

Introduction

Ethical practice is a fundamental concept and expectation for social workers and those with whom they work. As Jawad states in the above quote, ethics, also referred to as 'morality', is fundamental within many religions. As the director of a Scottish faith-based organization stated:

Voluntary agencies with a religious kind of history and background do have a – I mean I know with this agency, but I speak to other agencies as well – there's a real kind of moral imperative around what we do. . . . Local authorities don't in the same way do that and I think it's because faith-based agencies do believe – come from a kind of moral sort of point of our responsibility.

If this speaker is correct, one might readily conclude that ethical practice within faith-based organizations could be assumed and was a non-issue. However, as to what is considered ethical is frequently contested and there is the potential for disparate ethical stances within and between faith-based organizations, let alone between faith-based organizations and individuals or groups not working from a faith basis. This chapter will first consider notions of ethical practice by faith-based organizations before turning to explore some ethical concerns for social workers employed by faith-based organizations.

Ethical practice by faith-based organizations

Ethical practice by organizations, sometimes referred to as 'corporate social responsibility', may extend from ensuring that stakeholders are not harmed, to an obligation to act in ways which the organization contributes to the well-being of those it serves (Ozanne and Rose 2013). Stereotypically, in the case of faith-based organizations, this has frequently involved taking stances for or against particular practices or behaviours such that it has been proposed that 'the moral nature of a religious group is characterized not only by the practices it develops for observing fundamental imperatives but by those imperatives it recognizes and those it does not' (Battin 1990: 192).

Some of the most common ethical issues for faith-based organizations involve proscriptions around sexual behaviour and human reproduction, including sexual intercourse outside marriage, sexual relationships between persons of the same sex, contraception and termination of pregnancy. Medical interventions, including blood transfusions, use of donor organs and euthanasia, and substance use, including alcohol or stimulants such as caffeine, may be considered problematic within some religions. Furthermore, religious communities associated with faith-based organizations may have stances grounded in their beliefs about matters including spirit possession, infant circumcision, corporal punishment and religious-based practices such as male infant circumcision, as well as the rights of adults versus children and women versus men (Furness and Gilligan 2010a).

Ethical considerations vary between religions. For example, if an elderly person in care decided she no longer wanted to live and refused food, respect for autonomous choices may guide practitioners working in Protestant or Hindu settings, whereas the principle of sanctity of life would present issues in Catholic, Jewish and Muslim settings, all of which are religions which may consider such actions to be suicide, which is morally reprehensible (Linzer 2006). However, within a religion there can be very different inter-pretations as to what is ethical. For example, unlike many other branches of Christianity which are explicitly opposed (Quadagno and Rohlinger 2009), the Church of Sweden and the Church of Norway officially support abortion (Barbosa da Silva 2009). Nevertheless, there are those within these churches who oppose this. Hence, even social workers working from a similar religious basis may come with very different perspectives on so-called moral issues such as abortion:

> Whereas one social worker may cite the 'thou shall not kill' commandment as the reason to restrict a woman's right to choose,

another cites the God given endowment of humans to make choices, as reason to support a woman's right to choose.

(Ortiz 2003: 52)

In response to their particular beliefs, religious communities may deem it as not appropriate to provide particular services or only to provide them within limited parameters. For example, consistent with its understanding of Islamic principles, Islamic Relief will provide advice on family planning and distribute contraceptives but only to those who are married, except in situations where not to do so would be placing individuals at a high risk of harm (Palmer 2011). However, sometimes it is less clear-cut as to whether offering a specific service conflicts with religious beliefs, particularly when there are conflicting perspectives about 'conflicting political and religious views about individual and corporate responsibilities' (Furness and Gilligan 2012: 603).

In Australia in the late 1990s, it was anticipated that the country's first medically supervised injecting centre would be run by the Sisters of Charity Health Services, a major provider of drug treatment services in Sydney and part of the Roman Catholic Church. Under pressure from the Vatican which did not consider this an appropriate service in which the Catholic Church should be involved, the Sisters of Charity withdrew their involvement (MSIC 2013). However, this was not the end of faith-based involvement in such a service and when the Sydney Medically Supervised Injecting Centre [MSIC] opened in 2001 it was auspiced by the Uniting Church which at the time argued:

> Sometimes, in order to live in community with another person we must be prepared to tolerate actions with which we do not necessarily agree. The dilemma of the Church in the situation of drug addiction is no different to that faced by families with drug takers. Do they totally exclude the offending family member until he/she is rehabilitated or do they at least provide food and shelter and maintain the contact which, ultimately, can provide the environment for change?
>
> The critics of an MSIC will characterise it as a place of hopelessness and despair. Some critics of the MSIC argue that it is giving the message that there is no way out for the addict and that the best that can be done is to stop them from killing themselves. This is a false image of an MSIC. . . . Indeed, the MSIC will be rather an embodiment of Christian hope because it will say to the addict, even though we don't approve of your habit, and we all know that what you are doing is illegal outside this room, we will make a space for you to inject, because we believe that our first consideration is to keep you alive so that other things can be addressed later.

(Herbert and Talbot 2000)

Ethical considerations not only contribute to the decisions by faith-based organizations to commence new services but also to decisions about the future of existing services. Changes in legislation in 2007 had significant consequences for the adoption agencies associated with the Catholic Church in Britain. Whereas they had previously been able to set their own criteria for adoptive parents and could exclude couples not legally married or same-sex couples, such restrictions became illegal and organizations receiving public funding were required to change their assessment process to be in line with the legislation (St Andrew's Children's Society 2012). Believing this to be against Catholic notions of the family, some organizations advocated for an exemption from the requirement not to take into account sexual orientation of potential adoptive parents, while others decided to close their adoption services rather than comply with such requirements (Cosis Brown and Kershaw 2008). A third alternative was to adopt the new requirements and continue involvement in the field of adoption. At least one Catholic adoption agency in England decided not to follow the recommendation of their bishop that they cease involvement in adoption and fostering if they could not be exempted from placing children with unmarried or same-sex couples (White 2008). This organization now states in information to prospective adopters:

> We welcome enquiries from married or unmarried couples who have a stable long term relationship and who have made a life long commitment to one another, and we also welcome enquiries from single people. What is important is that adopters are positively motivated and able to meet the needs of children and provide a stable, loving home.
>
> (Caritas Care 2013a)

Having made a decision to continue as an adoption provider resulted in the agency losing its official status as a church organization (White 2008). Despite a rift with the bishop however, no longer being formally affiliated with the Catholic Church and having undergone a change of name, the organization retains a Christian identity (Caritas Care 2013b). A much more amicable separation was achieved by a Scottish organization which also chose to remain working in the field of adoption:

> Our close links to the Catholic community continue despite the formal relationship with the Church ending in 2010 when the Equality Regulations came into effect. Our former president, Cardinal O'Brien, is still a strong supporter of the work we do and we still receive support from many clergy in the Archdiocese of St. Andrews and Edinburgh.
>
> (St Andrew's Children's Society 2012: 8)

Each of the differing ways in which the Catholic adoption societies and their religious hierarchies responded to the changes in adoption legislation reflects an ethical imperative, with the key difference being whether providing a compromised service is regarded as better or worse than not providing a service at all (Hyde 2012). How seemingly similar organizations could make such different decisions about their future directions is a pertinent reminder that ethical decision-making in faith-based organizations may be context specific, with ethical imperatives:

> expressed in a general way rather than as a clear guidepost for ethical resolution. Additionally, these were superseded by other considerations such as regulations, funders, intra-organizational power dynamics, or principles derived from other reference points (such as faith). Thus, decisions regarding social work practice seem to be informed largely by non-social work values and procedures.
>
> (Hyde 2012: 363)

Decisions made may also reflect the different roles of various stakeholders in the organization when it comes to strategic decision-making (Hyde 2012). However, ethical practice in faith-based organizations does not just apply to strategic decision-making, but also to the values which underpin practice on a daily basis. When discussing their organizations, many of the research participants noted values such as integrity, compassion, social justice and dignity as occupying a central place in the organizational ethos (see also Jawad 2012b). For example, as one explained:

> I think the real strength of an organization like [organization] is their ethos and their Christian values of kind of compassion and love and social justice and that. I think that really drives it as an organization and there are other factors like business models and such like which drive it, but I think that's a real strength for it and other similar faith-based organizations, which isn't maybe always as strong in secular organizations.

A strong value in some faith-based organizations is hospitality. Comparing her organization to non-faith-based organizations, a social worker commented:

> In this organization, if we were having a meeting at lunchtime, inviting people to come to something at 12.30, we would always provide some lunch. . . . Someone told me the other day they went to [non-faith-based organization], for a meeting at 12.30 and they got a water jug and polystyrene cups. And I've been to other meetings where you haven't got offered anything.

Programmes within organizations are often funded in silos, but service users need to be treated holistically (Gardner 2011). Ethical practice at an organizational level can mean ensuring that once service users commence in a service the programmes they are assessed for are provided, even if funding received by the organization changes mid-programme. Referring to a programme in a non-faith-organization which had previously provided a mix of services, including medical and dental treatment along with counselling and life skills, one research participant noted how unethical it was to cease intervention mid-treatment:

> Anyway, [non-faith-based organization] have recently changed their brokerage, that the medical category of brokerage and the life skills category of brokerage have gone, and all you can now have is counselling. So that means you might have been halfway through some treatment for your teeth and the funding has just stopped. Now, I actually think that's unethical to do that, and I have said that. Now if that was in [faith-based organization] I don't think we would make that decision because I think we would have much greater principles in place and our values would say that you can't just suddenly stop that and you would have to find a way to get around that. So I guess for me, the fact that the organization has these values, the fact that they come from where they do, usually means for me that it is easier to make an ethical decision.

Funding shortages may also lead to ethical dilemmas as to where faith-based organizations should seek funding from. In Scotland, a social worker told of the expectations that non-government organizations seeking funding would apply to the National Lottery Commission, and may be ineligible for some funding sources if they have not applied for this:

> I don't go in the lottery right, because I think, I don't believe in gambling in general, and I think gambling can be particularly, with the more vulnerable people that we work with, can be quite negative for them. . . . I was involved in [organization] 10–15 years ago, they were saying quite clearly, 'We will not be involved in the national lottery and we won't accept national lottery money.' Which, right, I believe in that and I agree with that but the problem is that the government have changed the rules now and you can only get certain grants if you have actually applied for the lottery as well. So [organization] have now said, 'Well, as it stands, which way we will accept . . .', you know, so that they are wishing for their, what they are trained in, what their belief is so, and it's the fire to the nails, all the regulations get slightly, just diluted. It's not going away but slightly changed something.

Social work practice

Working for an organization with a strong value base can support and reinforce social workers' capacity to practise within their ethical framework, particularly if there is congruence between the organization's values and the social workers' code of ethics (Ortiz 2003) and especially if they are employed by an organization in their own faith tradition (Neagoe 2013). In response to a question about any tensions between his religious beliefs and understanding of social work, an Australian social worker replied, 'No, I never experienced that. I felt that they aligned quite well and certainly when I studied social work I felt that they fitted with my own ethics anyway. Having grown up in the [religion], that was simply a part of me.' Similarly, a social worker working in an organization from a different religious tradition said:

> I've always found them quite aligned and it could potentially be because I was from the faith that the agencies were, so there was a good synergy there. It might have been interesting for instance if I worked in an alternative faith-based agency that wasn't aligned to my denomination. There potentially could have been more issues in that scenario.

Whereas a professional code of ethics is binding on its members and is prescriptive in identifying what is appropriate behaviour by individuals, a code of practice for an individual organization may establish normative expectations of its staff. While this doesn't necessarily have to result in conflict for individuals who are expected to comply with both, it can do so, and there is the potential for this in faith-based organizations (Smith 1989). Hence, it may be necessary to recognize the different perspectives which underpin religious teaching and professional codes of ethics. It has been argued that the underlying philosophical bases of social work and Christianity differ such that tensions between the two would be expected if not inevitable, with contemporary social work often founded on secular humanist principles rather than on divine teaching (Stewart 2009). However, emphasizing apparent differences between religious and professional codes of ethics/practice can mask underlying similarities and the fact that both want what is best for individuals (Siporin 1986), whereas emphasizing the similarities may obscure the potential for conflict (Neagoe 2013). For example, it has been argued that both Catholic social teaching and social work codes of ethics respect the basic human rights of individuals and groups (Ebear *et al.* 2006; Himchak 2005) and that there is more convergence than divergence between these two influential dialogues

(Brenden 2007). A social worker working in a Catholic organization drew links between her professional ethics and Catholic social teaching:

> I don't know that there is a clash. I think they just come from different perspectives, but they are one and the same in lots of ways but are driven by different in saying Catholic social teaching, the agency values and that, that is coming from gospel values. Very rooted in the gospel I suppose, whereas, social work and the values within the code of practice and all that, is not necessarily.

Similarly, it has been noted that both Islamic (Ashencaen Crabtree *et al.* 2008) and Jewish (Guttmann and Cohen 1995) teachings are compatible with the principles of social work. Nevertheless, it is necessary to realize that ethical systems based on religious teachings do not necessarily provide day-to-day practice guidance for social workers or other professionals (Constable 2007). Ressler and Hodge (2003) in their interviews with 12 US social workers who identified as theologically conservative Christians found that all the respondents regarded their personal values as compatible with the values set out in the NASW Code of Ethics, i.e. service, social justice, dignity and worth of the person, importance of human relationships, integrity, and competence. Nevertheless, they recognized that others may not view their religiously based stances on some issues to be in concordance with ethical stances held by others within the profession. In other words, it is the interpretation not the principle which may lead to dissent.

On the other hand, there are practices in some religions which go against social work ethics, particularly around equality of treatment for women and people who don't identify as heterosexual, and it may be important that these are able to be addressed (Brenden 2007; Larson and Robertson 2007), especially when religious beliefs have been used to sanction violence:

> History demonstrates how spirituality, in the form of religion can be used to validate violence in the form of war and oppression of many kinds. Christianity has been problematic for many, endorsing missionary zeal that ignores the spirituality of others. We live still in a world where religious values are used to justify violence and to impose life limiting expectations on individuals and communities. This happens at many levels: continuing warfare in many parts of the world, tensions within communities where there is religious intolerance; an expectation, for example, that women remain married in spite of domestic violence; at policy and program levels such as whether funding should be provided for condoms in AIDS prone areas.
>
> (Gardner 2011: 20)

Social workers in faith-based organizations may report working around agency policies and practices to meet the needs of clients (Svare *et al.* 2007) and on a day-to-day basis have considerable autonomy which enables them to do so. As one social work manager explained, 'I often say to my staff that "look, you've got a level of autonomy in your role, use it . . . you've got a level of autonomy, you're all professionals and can make those choices"'.

The autonomous worker may recognize the ethical stance of their organization but determine that there are other moral imperatives which also need to be considered. Workers in a faith-based organization associated with a religion where sex outside marriage is not approved may nevertheless put aside their own disapproval and support individuals such as unmarried pregnant teenagers (Siporin 1986). Hence, when asked about whether there were ever any tensions between the values espoused by the organization and her understanding of social work, an experienced social worker in a Catholic organization responded:

> There are probably two answers to that. One would be the official answer and one would be the practice answer, I think. And it's probably most obvious in the area of youth when you are talking about contraception and a lot of talk about safe sex which . . . was more of a case of do what you need to do to educate the person and help them to make their own choices and to be safe and that sort of thing. And don't bring too much to our attention that there's a conflict in that. These days I think that the young person's welfare is first and foremost and whatever needs to happen to promote their welfare and give them choices.

When it's not possible to provide a service within their faith-based organization, social workers may refer a service user to another organization which can meet and address their needs. There will also be times when social workers may consider it necessary to explicitly challenge the organization's stance which may result in values being imposed upon service users (Neagoe 2013). For example, not permitting service users to consume alcohol may be consistent with some interpretations of religious teaching but impinging upon their freedom to make choices (Lake 2013). As a social worker in a faith-based organization which didn't approve of alcohol explains:

> If a client can't go shopping, I will catch a bus with them to wherever they need to go. One of the ethical dilemmas that I had at one stage, and it was a really interesting one too, one of my clients wanted me to take him to an alcohol store to buy alcohol. Now [organization] has a no-alcohol policy. So I was instructed not to take my client to an alcohol shop. Now it's going back a fair while, and my response to that was 'Why is that?' Because the [organization] doesn't believe in drinking but how is that relevant to taking a client and his choice? He's not going to drink in front of me, so for me there's a lot of ethical

dilemma around that. Do I respect the client's individuality or do I have to abide by the [organization's] guidelines? . . .

Well I offset that by saying that the guy has never been shopping. He's actually stepped outside his house and started to address social inclusion. This is about social inclusion which is what we are about and I argued the point and I won.

There may however be times when social workers in faith-based organizations are horrified by the requests of service users. For example, a Scottish social worker talked about a residential setting for adults, where service users with learning difficulties had been known to request the services of commercial sex workers. Such requests raise issues as to what is the organization's limits of responsibility when person-centred planning is expected to be a key principle in social work practice:

Our organization does sometimes have issues with . . . members of staff who are asked by service users, not just with learning difficulties, but with difficulties about, to provide them with prostitutes and things like that. And the first time that came up it was like, 'What will God say?' And that is quite clear, that is offensive, they don't do it. But the, I think that is what can be difficult being within a Christian organization and actually providing someone with what they best need for their needs if that doesn't 100 per cent tie in with your own faith. But I think that happens in any organization whether you are a Christian organization or not. . . . But I mean there was a real panic, what do you do? Will people say that we are being bad because we are Christians, or see that we are actually taking a step to protect these vulnerable adults? Which is more of what was being done rather than because we are Christian, because we believe what should be done.

When self-determination potentially conflicts with religious values, social workers may need to ensure that they are not perceived as promoting a religious viewpoint or the need for religious conversion. Ethical practice is non-discriminatory and service provision should not be contingent upon receptivity to any efforts at proselytizing (De Cordier 2009), although it is just as important that social workers are not coerced into taking or supporting actions which they regard as unethical. Attempts to limit self-determination by service users may also come from individuals outside the organization who make it known as to what they expect from a faith-based organization. For example, a social worker in a faith-based organization which offers relationship counselling may find abusive spouses expecting them to uphold religious teachings which promote marriage as an inviolable contract (Gardner 2011). In addition to self-determination, other potential clashes between social work and religious values have been identified in respect of notions of informed consent and confidentiality (Battin 1990).

In addition to the specific ethical issues which emerge directly from working in a faith-based organization, social workers in faith-based organizations also experience many ethical issues with social workers employed in other sectors. One such issue is the involvement of unqualified staff in case work or counselling roles. Although many faith-based organizations have a high regard for professionalism and may regard it as a hallmark of ethical practice (Ferris 2011), others have paid unqualified staff or volunteers who may lack knowledge of what is regarded as best practice and ethical practice in their field (Charnley 2007; Conradson 2011). As one Australian social worker explained:

> Interesting enough we have a manager who de-professionalized case management a few years ago. Their work ethics weren't up to our standard for some of the workers; just the way they dealt with clients, they were quite abrupt. They told them 'This is how it's going to be.' As opposed to working with the client, asking them what they need.

While social workers in any setting may find themselves working with services users who have experienced a religious conversion, service users may be more open to disclosing this to staff in a faith-based organization, particularly one aligned with their new-found religion. At the same time, social workers, particularly those who do not want to be seen as in any way encouraging such a conversion, even if privately they regard it as positive, may be uneasy in discussing this. As to what is the role of the professional worker when a service user has a religious conversion, Maxine Green (2010) provides the following guidance, which is applicable both within and outside faith-based organizations:

> What is important is that the concept of conversion is not necessarily positive or negative. It is possible to assess the impact that conversion has on people's lives and to make judgements based on assessing their subsequent behaviour against particular expectations. For example, as a result of conversion, are people happier, and do they have more or less control over their lives?
>
> (Green 2010: 124)

Social workers may also encounter service users who have been subjected to exorcisms or other religious interventions that have sought to rid them of some form of evil spirit which has either not been effective or has increased their level of disturbance (Coyte 2007). One of the most horrific cases of child abuse which has received widespread reporting in recent years is the case of Victoria Climbié, who died at 8 years of age in London in 2000. The previous year she was sent from the Ivory Coast to live with a relative, initially in France, before moving to London. Although she suffered from an illness which caused incontinence, this was interpreted by her carers as wilful behaviour caused by evil spirits. As punishment she was kept in an empty bath, tied up in a bag containing her own excrement and forced to eat cold food. The advice from the pastor of a local church was that Victoria's problematic behaviour could be solved by prayer. When the condition subsequently returned, the same pastor suggested that insufficient care had been taken, hence allowing the evil spirit to return. Some months later she was taken to a second church where the pastor also diagnosed spirit possession as the problem which needed curing (Laming 2003). Although the social workers involved with Victoria Climbié were employed in statutory agencies and not by faith-based organizations, Gilligan (2010) has proposed spirit possession as one of the key moral issues which needs to be addressed in respect of social work in faith-based organizations. However, beliefs in spirit possession do not necessarily result in harm (Briggs *et al.* 2011), and the number of cases of child abuse associated with spirit possession presenting themselves to social workers in any setting is very low (Briggs *et al.* 2011; Gilligan 2008). In all likelihood a social worker in a faith-based organization may never encounter a case, but when it does occur this may well be one issue when individual social workers find they cannot reconcile religious beliefs with their social work values.

Conclusion

There may be multiple and contradictory perspectives on what is considered ethical practice when considering service provision by faith-based welfare organizations, especially when organizations are working from a supposedly similar value basis in similar situations such as the Catholic adoption agencies in Britain. Not only has this issue created schisms in the social work community between those who are anti-homosexual and those who are anti-religious (Melville-Wiseman 2013) but it has opened up public debate as to the contemporary relevance of the so-called ethical stance taken by some faith-based organizations. At the same time that some faith-based organizations are taking issue with increasingly prevailing community values which tolerate a wide range of sexual identities and lifestyles beyond heterosexual marriage,

> Others are sceptical about a public role for faiths on the grounds of a perception of their tendency to assert moral superiority by appeal to imagined deities, coupled with self-justifying discrimination expressed in sexism, racism and homophobia.
>
> (Dinham 2012a: 8)

Working for a faith-based organization can indeed create challenges for ethical practice (Charnley 2007) and, prior to undertaking this research, social workers employed in other organizations often commented to the author that there would be too many ethical issues to overcome and that it would make employment in a faith-based organization difficult. Hence, social workers employed in faith-based organizations are more likely to be those who are able to negotiate the ethical issues associated with employment in this setting:

> The pragmatic reality is that when one chooses to work for any institution, whether Catholic, Dutch Reformed, Jewish, Muslim, or one in the public sector, the employment contract stipulates the practice arena and its limitations. If a social worker cannot find a balance point between her or his own values, the expectations of the profession's values upon them in the workplace and the expectations of the workplace, the logical choice is not to work in the setting.
>
> (Ebear *et al.* 2008: 191)

It is not that ethical issues do not emerge for social workers in faith-based organizations which might clash with the values of their employer but how they resolve these issues. Several of the research participants demonstrated an adeptness for doing what they believe is in the best interests of service users, which at times may involve taking a stance contra to what one might expect for an organization of a particular religious disposition.

Social work in faith-based organizations will probably raise difficult ethical issues for individuals, organizations and whole societies. However, this is perhaps no more so than when faith-based organizations are considered to have engaged in unethical practices at a systemic level, which will be the focus of Chapter 7.

7

CONTROVERSIES

XX is a holy man –
He goes to church on Sunday.
He prays to God to give him strength
To batter kids on Monday.

(Quoted in Shaw 2011: 50)

Introduction

Rhymes such as the one above, repeated by children in a Scottish residential home, have too often been uncritically dismissed by adults as untruths or phantasy. However, in many countries, the allegations of children about abuse can no longer be ignored. Scandals involving physical, mental and sexual abuse of children in their care have highlighted the high expectations in which societies hold faith-based organizations along with histories of highly problematic agency practices. Moreover, as alleged cases of child abuse are particularly newsworthy when the accused are supposedly upstanding citizens such as religious officials (Cheit *et al.* 2010), there are few members of the community who are unaware of claims of abuse within faith-based organizations and lacking in opinions about such claims.

There has been much written about abusive practices within religious organizations and communities, and especially sexual abuse by clergy within the Catholic Church. However, the focus of this chapter is confined to welfare provision by faith-based organizations and explores some of the ways in which certain faith-based organizations have been revealed to have engaged in abusive practices, often sustained over long periods of time. In particular the chapter will commence by considering evidence from official inquiries in Ireland and Scotland. In each of these inquiries there is no question of abuse not occurring, but they also shed light on the circumstances which enabled abuse to flourish. This chapter then goes on to identify some responses by faith-based organizations to these issues and the challenges for contemporary social workers in faith-based organizations in light of public recognition that faith-based organizations may be deeply flawed.

The Commission to Inquire into Child Abuse (CICA)

Perhaps the most comprehensive inquiry into abusive behaviour in religious institutions is the Commission to Inquire into Child Abuse (CICA), more commonly known as the *Ryan Report*, commissioned by the Irish government in 1999 to investigate the extent and effects of abuse on children from 1936 onward. Evidence of abuse while in care was provided by 1,090 persons, with many reporting multiple forms of abuse. The findings, published in May 2009 and consisting of five volumes containing more than 2,500 pages, report on abuse which happened in 216 schools and residential settings run by several Catholic religious orders (CICA 2009). Shocking accounts of physical and emotional abuse, as well as neglect and sexual abuse, being inflicted on girls and boys are provided. Readers of the *Ryan Report* learn that:

> Irish industrial and reform schools were based upon a philosophy of dehumanization that subjected the bodies and minds of their inmates to regimes of systematic violence. These human rights crimes were not committed by a totalitarian state, but primarily by church organizations in the name of charity in a society that purported to be democratic.
>
> (Powell *et al.* 2013: 21)

Although these institutions employed lay staff, many of the reported accounts involved perpetrators who were members of religious orders. The CICA and other recent reports about abuse by Catholic clergy or within Catholic settings in Ireland have identified a situation in which the Catholic Church and government authorities were 'enmeshed' (Pilgrim 2012: 410) such that reports of abuse to state authorities were frequently not investigated. Sometimes the police informed the church authorities about complaints but left any action to the relevant bishop, who frequently failed to follow up the complaint (Pilgrim 2011, 2012).

Many of the recruits to religious orders which ran the institutions began religious life as young as 14, i.e. when still children, and not mature adults. For many from poor families, this was the only way of continuing their education (Pilgrim 2012). However, while encouraging obedience and a lack of questioning of religious authorities (McLoone-Richards 2012), the culture of the religious orders was often not conducive to facilitating sexual and emotional maturity (Pilgrim 2012), especially for those who had themselves grown up with poor experiences of parenting (McLoone-Richards 2012). These factors, combined with religious teachings which emphasized physical punishment as being good for the soul (Pilgrim 2012), along with geographic and intellectual isolation of many of the institutions where children were cared for (Pilgrim 2011), led to a situation in which in retrospect it is not unsurprising that the abuse of children was able to occur. Many former residents reported physical punishments, including:

> punching, flogging, assault and bodily attacks, hitting with the hand, kicking, ear pulling, hair pulling, head shaving, beating on the soles of the feet, burning, scalding, stabbing, severe beatings with or without clothes, being made to kneel and stand in fixed positions for lengthy periods, made to sleep outside overnight, being forced into cold or excessively hot baths and showers, hosed down with cold water before being beaten, beaten while hanging from hooks on the wall, being set upon by dogs, being restrained in order to be beaten, physical assaults by more than one person, and having objects thrown at them.
>
> (CICA 2009: Volume 3, paragraph 7.16)

Such punishments could be administered without any reason and the reasons given for punishment often betrayed a fundamental knowledge of the essence of normal childhood behaviour and development:

> In addition to reports of what appeared to be indiscriminate violence, witnesses reported being beaten for other reasons, including: bed-wetting and soiling, inattention in the classroom, left-handedness, stammering, not knowing lessons, disclosing physical and/or sexual abuse, absconding, 'stealing' food, talking in line, delay in obeying an instruction, '*looking the wrong way*' at a staff member, attending the infirmary, complaining of feeling unwell, general wear and tear on clothing and footwear, talking at meals or in bed, talking to girls, playing soccer, losing a game against an outside team, perceived sexual thoughts or actions and not being able to carry out work tasks quickly and properly.
>
> (CICA 2009: Volume 3, paragraph 7.28)

Furthermore, a poor understanding of child development along with staff shortages frequently resulted in inadequate supervision, and children being left to care for each other:

> Witness accounts of inadequate supervision and lack of appropriate care and protection were heard in relation to all decades. Witnesses described supervision ranging from 'patrolling' yards with sticks and

the regimented use of a whistle, to young children being left in the care of older residents without any supervising adult staff. '*If the babies were crying some boys would be designated to get up and have a look, I remember turning them around or moving them. What were they doing letting an 8 year old boy do that?*' Large numbers of residents were routinely under the supervision of a single staff member or other co-residents in areas including classrooms, trade shops, farms, bogs, dormitories, refectories and yards. '*I recall only 2 Brothers being in charge of 200 boys; the bullies were given a free rein.*'

(CICA 2009: Volume 3, paragraph 7.198)

Some former residents acknowledged the staff shortages and felt that perhaps staff had done the best they could do for the children in their care:

A small number of witnesses were appreciative of the staff that cared for them even though they wished to make clear that they also experienced abuse in the Schools. '*They gave children a great life, they did not mean what they did, no matter how cruel they were, where would I have been without them?*' Some witnesses expressed the view that the religious and lay staff in charge of them probably did the best they could under difficult circumstances and four witnesses said that in retrospect, they appreciated the sense of security provided by being contained in an institutional environment when they were young.

(CICA 2009: Volume 3, paragraph 10.30)

Poor hygiene, lack of appropriate clothing and bedding, and inadequate medical and dental services were common complaints. For some adolescent girls, puberty was marked with being beaten or humiliated when they commenced menstruating and needed to access sanitary protection or grew breasts and needed bras. To what extent this reflects deliberately malicious behaviour by staff, or the consequences of staff members who often had no training or qualifications to care for children is unknown. However, it is possible that failure to provide even basic living requirements could in part also reflect the financial resources available to some institutions. In Ireland, the state needed but could not afford to properly resource the institutions which the Church was prepared to run for children needing care (McLoone-Richards 2012), and it is probable that a consequence of this was insufficient and poor-quality food being a common complaint of former residents:

Some witnesses reported having so little to eat that at times they were starving. The Committee heard many reports from witnesses of attempts to satisfy their hunger by 'raiding' the garden, orchard and kitchens for extra food, eating grasses, dandelion, hawthorn, sorrel leaves and wild berries found while out on walks and while working in the fields. Witnesses also reported taking food from slop buckets, potatoes and other feed prepared for pigs, skimmed milk for calves and dried animal feed in the farmyards. Bread dipped in dripping and shell cocoa described by one witness as '*unsweetened sludge*' was a standard part of the diet recounted by witnesses discharged in the years before the 1960s.

(CICA 2009: Volume 3, paragraph 7.163)

For some, not eating was preferable to consuming what was served, although refusal to eat what was provided could result in punishment or being forcibly fed. Failure to provide for the needs of individual children constitutes emotional abuse and reflects an 'atmosphere of fear' which was 'pervasive and systemic' (CICA 2009: Volume 3, paragraph 7.214). Unlike much of the physical or sexual abuse which could be attributed to specific individuals, emotional abuse was often the consequence of regimented institutional processes, including being denied contact with or information about family members. Denial of identity went as far for some children as being known as a number rather than by name or not having birthdays recognized let alone celebrated, and in the longer term having insufficient information in order to obtain a passport.

Large-scale institutional care of children in previous generations often resulted in the true potential of children not being realized and in some cases denied adequate education (Murray *et al.* 2009), and is another form of abuse (Smith 2010):

> The neglect of education was reported by many witnesses who referred to the lack of adequate teaching and support for learning. Witnesses consistently reported that the fear of abuse, having to work for the institution and lack of attention to their learning difficulties contributed to the overall neglect of their education.
>
> Sixty nine (69) witnesses reported being illiterate when they were discharged from the Schools and many others acknowledged that poor literacy and numeracy skills had been a serious impediment in their subsequent lives. Two hundred and sixty three (263) witnesses (64%) reported that they were discharged from the School system without sitting for their Primary Certificate.
>
> (CICA 2009: Volume 3, paragraphs 7.185–186)

While in retrospect it is clear that the care of children by the Catholic Church in Ireland over many decades was deeply problematic, questions must also be asked about the acquiescing of the state and its dereliction of duty of care towards Ireland's children. The enmeshment which enabled lack of action about complaints of abuse when church officials were involved seems also to apply to the lack of state supervision of care institutions. The CICA report notes a lack of rigour such that inspections of institutions didn't occur, or were done in such a cursory way that inspectors were unwilling or unable to obtain a realistic view of life for children being cared for. Furthermore, when inspections did occur, children's views were discounted, if they were heard at all (Powell *et al.* 2013).

Stories of physical, sexual and emotional abuse of children who spent their formative years in institutions run by religious groups are not uncommon, but the experience cannot be generalized across all children even in one institution with many others having positive experiences and in some instances believing it to be much better than what had been on offer from their blood families (Murray *et al.* 2009). Hence,

> Accounts of care, kindness, attention and support provided by individual religious and lay staff were given in evidence by both male and female witnesses. Such experiences included incidents and encounters both within the School and in the wider community.
> (CICA 2009: Volume 3, paragraph 10.02)

As critics have noted, the *Ryan Report* is not without its shortcomings, with a key criticism being that perpetrators of abuse have been allowed to remain anonymous (Powell *et al.* 2013). However, the strength of the inquiry was that it enabled long-silenced voices to at last be heard and acknowledged within Irish society. Arguably Rachel Lev's comments in respect of the need to provide opportunities within the American Jewish community to individuals who have experienced abuse also apply to former child residents of Catholic institutions in Ireland:

> We bear witness in part by listening to survivor stories. Then we address the questions: How do we help people heal? What do we do to stop these abuses? Where do we start? Simple answers will not work. Blaming and shaming won't work even though they're tempting. Healing and prevention happen together when we listen to the stories that must be told, then share resources and a commitment to peaceful relationships. Healing comes when we 'shine the light' on what is, what was, and what needs to be.
> (Lev 2003: xxvii)

Quarriers

While the CICA was collecting evidence in Ireland from former child residents, allegations of abuse having occurred in residential childcare settings in Scotland gained prominence. Unlike Ireland where agencies of the Catholic Church were the key providers of residential care, many of the complaints in Scotland came from former residents of homes based on

Protestant religious beliefs, but not necessarily with a formal religious affiliation, such as Quarriers. A former resident of Quarriers Village in Scotland recalls recognizing his own experience in the stories emerging of abuse in Catholic institutions in Ireland:

> I came forward because I felt I was holding it in myself and folk should really know what goes on behind closed doors. . . . It was not a home, more like a prison. You were not even allowed to walk on the grass. When the priests' thing came out, I thought 'That happened to me' to the point where I started to commit suicide. I was frightened to go into a room with any grown-up. The only man I would have trusted was one of my teachers.
>
> (Former Quarriers resident, in Shaw 2011: 20)

In response to mounting public pressure, the Scottish Executive commissioned a systematic review examining the regulatory framework governing care of children outside the home in Scotland from 1950 to 1995 (Smith *et al.* 2012). Much of the information considered in this review involved documentary evidence, although this was supplemented by evidence provided by former residents and staff (Shaw 2007). However, the focus on systems with no findings pertaining to individual persons or institutions was considered an inadequate response to the concerns raised by former residents (Smith *et al.* 2012). Rather than attempt an inquiry which would consider the concerns in all institutions, in 2009 the Scottish government commissioned a further review which had become known as *Time To Be Heard* and focusing on Quarriers, a large residential setting near Glasgow (Shaw 2011).

In 1871, William Quarrier, a Scottish businessman, established the Orphan Homes of Scotland in the countryside 15 miles from Glasgow, an organization known today as Quarriers. Originally planned to have 10 houses, over time an almost self-contained village grew, with its own school, church, hospital, fire station and farm, and more than 40 cottages housing the children. At its peak it housed some 1,500 children, who had little contact with the outside world while residing in the village. Between 1871 and its closing in the late 1980s, 30,000 children were accommodated at Quarriers Village at some point in their childhood, and often for many years. Hence, it was considered that focusing on this one organization might provide a representative case study of children's experiences of abuse in Scottish residential facilities for children. Furthermore, since 2001 there have been criminal convictions against six former Quarriers staff which were related to abuse perpetrated while a Quarriers employee (Shaw 2011).

Quarriers has never been formally auspiced by any of the churches in Scotland but was instilled with the beliefs of its Protestant founder. While it no longer has a Christian identity, during the period when it provided residential care in the village, Quarriers not only had an explicitly Christian ethos but it maintained an expectation that staff employed there would be practising Christians. As the commissioner in charge of the *Time To Be Heard* review subsequently reflected:

> House parents were recruited principally on the strength of their Christian character and practice. But despite that some seem to have fallen far short in providing the standard of care expected and to which the children were entitled. What we heard suggests that some of them lacked the personality, temperament, skill or integrity to care for the children appropriately.
>
> (Shaw 2011: 18)

This was certainly the lived experience of some former residents, as one resident who lived at Quarriers Village in the 1950s recalled:

> Religion was pushed down our throats. I liked the church. It was a safe place. The kids were singing. But I'm not religious today. I learned to be very fearful in that place. You got scared because there were people who could hurt you. The orphanage was cruel, unloving and it just shaped me and shaped my life.
>
> (Former resident of Quarriers, in Shaw 2011: 22)

The lack of screening of care providers other than that they professed to be Christian had serious consequences for some children who were placed in the care of adults who believed it their right to sexually abuse the children. A number of former residents reported experiencing sexual abuse to the *Time To Be Heard* inquiry and, as one who resided at Quarriers in the 1960s told the commissioners:

> He [my house father] used to say 'Who will you tell? Nobody will believe you.' He also told me to remember that, when I left, my sisters would still be in Quarriers. . . . You go to the grave with it, no matter how much therapy you get. It's not a healthy environment for a child. You wish you could erase it, but you can't. Quarriers was a paradise for paedophiles. I don't think they were properly screened or supervised. The only qualification was that you were a regular church-goer and you liked children.
>
> (Former Quarriers resident, in Shaw 2011: 26)

A culture that enabled abuse to flourish at Quarriers Village is not dissimilar to that which existed in some residential care settings run by the statutory sector across the UK (Stein 2006). Not only was there inadequate supervision by the state in Scotland of organizations which cared for children on its behalf (Shaw 2007), but evidence of attempts by management to alter the culture at Quarriers Village tended to be ineffective. Furthermore, staff often perpetuated myths that the children living in care were essentially immoral and lacking the virtues of those who were responsible for their care. As the commissioner in charge of the *Time To Be Heard* inquiry noted, this resulted in a situation where:

> There was a feeling that people who are allegedly Christian must be good. They can't have all these allegations against them. Some kids will make up stories, but not every kid every time. . . . It was a sign of the times that kids were not listened to – so they got away with it. It can't be easy, with 500 kids, to listen to every kid and believe every kid.
>
> (Shaw 2011: 30)

In respect of concerns about the lack of qualifications of childcare staff during the period when Quarriers Village housed children, it has been noted that in Scotland the regulatory frameworks with which residential childcare facilities had to comply made little or no reference to formal qualifications or other qualities which might be expected of care staff, or of standards of care which should be provided. Hence, what may now be seen as irresponsible staffing practices by Quarriers were similar to those then operating in other Scottish residential childcare facilities (Shaw 2007).

In 2001, on the day of the first verdict against a former staff member for sexual abuse of children living at Quarriers Village, the organization made a public apology which acknowledged that dreadful things had occurred to children in care which ought not to have happened. Although not yet public knowledge, Quarriers management were aware that the police were then investigating complaints against other former employees, which did subsequently result in convictions. Quarriers also set up a telephone hotline which former residents could ring to discuss concerns about abuse they may have experienced and seek appropriate advice, and established an after-care service which could assist former residents access their files and discuss the contents (Magnusson 2006).

Like the CICA in Ireland, the *Time To Be Heard* inquiry has been criticized on the basis of a methodology which in all likelihood has exaggerated the levels of abuse which occurred at Quarriers (Smith *et al.* 2012). Reviews of institutional abuse have often resulted in 'privileging narratives of suffering' (Smith 2010: 309), and the experiences of children for whom living in faith-based organizations was a positive experience have largely gone unnoticed (Murray *et al.* 2009). At Quarriers Village each residential unit was essentially a fiefdom and, depending on their luck, children were assigned to a cottage where they might be either well cared for or abused

(Shaw 2011). As one former resident of Quarriers told the commissioners at the *Time To Be Heard* inquiry:

> I came here because I didnae want someone to be painting Quarriers as a bad place. I wanted to make sure someone spoke up for the good side. Quarriers done good by me. You're going to get horror stories in every walk of life. The only bad thing for me was going to church twice on Sundays and Sunday afternoon clubs.
>
> (Former Quarriers resident, in Shaw 2011: 30)

While it will not be possible to ascertain just how prevalent abuse was at Quarriers Village, one can nevertheless be certain that having a faith basis did not necessarily protect children placed there from physical, sexual or emotional abuse. However, this is not the only reason why from a twenty-first-century viewpoint Quarriers was historically an organization which has been associated with controversies. Quarriers was one of several British organizations involved in the care of children between the 1870s and 1967 which altogether sent approximately 150,000 children overseas to begin new lives in Australia, Canada, New Zealand, Rhodesia (now Zimbabwe) and South Africa. Quarriers alone sent 7,000 children abroad between 1872 and the 1930s, with 35 per cent of children admitted to Quarriers during this period leaving as child emigrants. In recent years it has been estimated that 200,000 Canadians are descended from the child migrants from Quarriers (Magnusson 2006). William Quarrier himself genuinely believed that emigration to Canada was in the best interests of many of the children who came into his institution:

> For Quarrier, emigration was not just a convenient means of clearing Glasgow's streets of waif and strays; of course it was clear that his Glasgow Homes had limited accommodation and training facilities for the children and that emigration was in the best interests of his children and that Canada was truly a land of opportunity, where boys and girls could make a good future for themselves in a new, eager country which needed them.
>
> (Magnusson 2006: 68)

While the feedback received by Quarrier was that emigration had been a positive experience for the Scottish children sent from his homes, within a few years *The Glasgow Herald* newspaper was expressing concerns about child emigration. Sadly, those concerns were subsequently validated. Many child emigrants ended up in situations that were even less satisfactory and more abusive than the care facilities where they had been living in Britain (Sen *et al.* 2007), with very little, if any, checking of prospective caregivers in Canada (Magnusson 2006). It has also been established that many children emigrated believing their parents to be dead when this was not the case (Sen *et al.* 2007), and that it was not uncommon for some members of a sibling group to go to Canada while their brothers or sisters remained in Scotland. However, even siblings who went together to Canada were often separated soon after arrival. Furthermore, although they may have agreed to go, few children realized what they were agreeing to (Magnusson 2006). James McCallum, who was sent to Canada from Quarriers in the 1920s, has recalled that:

> I was asked if I wanted to go to Canada but I cannot remember by whom, and my answer 'yes' was just an impulse, as up to that moment I had not dreamed of going anywhere, especially Canada.
>
> There were no preparations for us prior to departure. No lectures, talks or anything what would prepare us for a new and strange life in Canada. . . .
>
> The Orphan Homes owned two buses, one large and one small, and we were taken to the ship in the big bus. It was the custom for all boys and girls to line the road leading to the main gates and cheer us on our way. I can remember leaning out of the bus trying to spot my sister in the crowd and screaming her name so that she would notice me. As we drove out of the gates I had a lump in my throat that had nothing to do with the Orphan Homes. It was for this little ten-year-old girl whom I suddenly realised I was leaving behind, possibly never to see again.
>
> (James McAllum, in Magnusson 2006: 87)

Quarriers no longer runs a residential village and has evolved into a twenty-first-century modern welfare organization offering a range of programmes, including some residential care for children. To what extent its current work is affected by the negative legacies of its work in both the village and through child emigration is unknown, but it is certainly not the only welfare organization emerging out of Christian philanthropy which became involved in child migration. One of the key organizations involved in child migration were Barnardos (Jupp 2009) which now advertise themselves 'As the UK's leading children's charity' (Barnardos 2013).

Responses by faith-based organizations

Many of the concerns raised by the *Ryan Report* in Ireland and the *Time To Be Heard* inquiry into Quarriers in Scotland were not unique to those settings. In summing up their interviews with 40 Australian adults who had spent at least part of their childhood living in Catholic institutions, Murray *et al.* concluded:

> Among these 40 Australians there were those who described their experiences of care as positive and who said they had stood them in good stead for their subsequent lives. Others, while acknowledging that some aspects of institutional care were less than perfect, pointed out that their lives, had they stayed in their home with their family, may not have turned out as well. Some believed that the orphanage staff did the best they could under difficult conditions; others again recalled experiencing severe abuse, poor education, and an environment that was lacking in care and emotional warmth, and these negative experiences were to have lifelong effects.
>
> (Murray *et al.* 2009: 172)

Long-term consequences of institutional abuse include low levels of educational attainment, difficulties in forming and maintaining relationships, lack of knowledge about parenting and running a home, and poor dental health (Murray *et al.* 2009). Furthermore, in Canada and Australia it is now accepted that residential childcare facilities run by churches in previous eras frequently alienated indigenous people from their culture and traditions (Schwartz *et al.* 2008; Wilson 1997).

Although faith-based organizations may prioritize their own needs – including maintaining their reputations – over the needs of service users (Gilligan 2010), many have in fact changed their ways of working so as to be more responsive to the needs of former service users and have adopted pro-active practices to reduce the likelihood of abuse happening in the future.

Responding to the needs of former service users

Apologies and compensation have been paid to some who were abused by religious institutions during childhood (Murray *et al.* 2009). However, as the experience in Ireland demonstrates, paying compensation is not the same as making an apology. Eighteen Catholic religious orders in Ireland agreed to contribute to a fund to compensate former child residents who had experienced abuse while in care. However, cynics have suggested that in some instances orders agreed to contribute to the fund not out of remorse but because it would grant them immunity from further legal action:

> It might have been thought that Congregations who contributed to the fund were in effect conceding that there had been some abuse in their institutions. The agreement did not require them to do so, but the mere fact of payment into the fund, in return for an indemnity in respect of

any actions that might be taken, could have been regarded as an expression of some kind of admission or acknowledgement, but it was said not to be the case.

The position with regard to apologies was more complicated. Some Congregations issued apologies and some did not. Those that issued apologies used a variety of different expressions. Through their spokespersons, they testified to the good intentions that lay behind the apologies. Some of the apologies were more effective than others in meeting the needs of survivor groups.

(CICA 2009: Volume 1, paragraphs 1.76–77)

Nevertheless, there are some faith-based organizations that have made serious attempts to confront their pasts and seek to make what redress is possible. An Australian research participant working in a faith-based organization which can trace its history back more than 100 years spoke of how:

[Organization's] leadership has talked a lot about how we have failed people as an organization in the past, and some reference to some dark things which have happened in the name of the orders. And I think a genuine desire to want to do anything in our power to make right the wrongs of the past. . . . The organization does a lot of work with past residents and acknowledging the abuse that has happened and the care practices of the past that wouldn't be acceptable today. And I think that's a credit to the organization that we've tried to be upfront and honest about that and taken responsibility for those sensitive things that have happened.

For the former child residents in Ireland and Quarriers Village, accessing their records was often a fraught experience as it has been elsewhere (Wilson 1997). If in fact they were successful in retrieving information relating to their time in care, it was often the result of a bureaucratic process rather than a process which acknowledged their vulnerability at this time. Hence, the *Time To Be Heard* inquiry recommended that service providers should:

*   Develop record management plans that are fit for purpose – and provide for historical records.
*   Take stock of and safeguard their historical records to help former residents make sense of their childhoods and remember more.
*   Provide skilled assistance and supportive arrangements to those former residents who are seeking information about themselves or about the institution that was their 'home'.
*   Anticipate surprise and shock for some former residents when they gain access to their records and provide support and empathy.

(Shaw 2011: 106)

The last two of the above bullet points strongly suggest a role for social workers to be involved in providing such a service. As a social worker who works in a faith-based organization where such a service exists commented:

> It was really clear that there needed to be a place to remember the past, a place to look after the records from the past, but more importantly, a place where people who grew up in the original homes and orphanages could access their story, access their records and begin the process of reconnection with their family. . . .
>
> A lot of people are much older when they make the decision to search for their records, when they make that decision to go on a search to understand more about their identity. So people approach it in very in-depth ways or in very shallow ways, depending on how much it is that they want to learn and how much they want to find separate family members. And most people are older, they are 50, 60, 70, 80 that contact. Sometimes whole families who were in care come in at similar times or sometimes our work with one family member leads to the rest of the family members coming in. It's very measured work. It's working with people that are apprehensive about going on a journey but are very willing participants.

As care practices and standards have often changed substantially since a person was in care, particularly if that was several decades ago, the social work role may include needing to contextualize the information available in the records, explain gaps, and act as the organization's listening ear to former service users who are distressed, angry or confused by what is revealed.

For participants in the *Time To Be Heard* inquiry, one of the things they had been seeking in their personal files was photographs of themselves as children. However, files typically included few if any photographs, but as there were numerous photographs in publications and the Quarriers archives the commissioners recommended an archive be developed which could be accessed by former residents (Shaw 2011). Furthermore, where possible, former residents who wish to are welcome to visit where they once lived, even if the buildings have been repurposed by the organization to be offices or have other uses (Murray *et al.* 2009; Shaw 2011). Even organizations which have gained a level of notoriety will have former residents with good memories who wish to maintain a connection or reconnect with some aspects of their life in care. As David, a former resident in a Catholic children's home in the United Kingdom recalls, in a far from perfect institution there were nevertheless some very good individuals who worked there:

> There were people who really cared and that shone through; and there were people who didn't care and that also shone through. There were

people that protected you, and people that abused you (and I use the term in the broadest sense). There was a nun who was the head of our children's home who was very, very fair, and kind, but not in a 'goody-goody' way – she was a just person, and she offered us protection. There were lots of things I would criticise about that children's home, although I would say it was of its time, but she stands out as being a very protective figure. There was no understanding of children's rights or children's voices at that time; we were at the mercy of lots of different forces – but she was a just person.

(In Cree and Davis 2007: 87)

New ways of working

Despite encountering often considerable obstacles to change (Murray *et al.* 2009), many faith-based organizations which have histories of controversies are almost unrecognizable from their predecessors. Even if the name has continued unchanged, chances are that working practices are unrecognizable from a few decades ago. In particular, as with other providers of welfare services, faith-based organizations are now subject to numerous standards and regulations. An Australian social worker reflecting on such changes said:

> Unquestionably there were abuses and hurts and all of that, but there were also you know, for some of the people that were there it was their home and they loved it, and they had some really good staff caring for them. So it's certainly a challenge and I don't think that current clients feel – I don't think anyone currently is concerned, or not me, would be concerned by that, but it's certainly a difficult chapter in our history. And does it make us more vigilant? I don't know. I mean, there are so many standards and regulations now that we are as vigilant as the next organization.

A common theme in both the *Ryan Report* and *Time To Be Heard* was a lack of human resource procedures for the selection and management of staff but the regimes for selecting staff in many contemporary faith-based organizations are far more rigorous than in previous eras. As a social worker employed in an organization which has been providing care since the nineteenth century commented:

> And I guess that the learning from those have placed a big responsibility on us to do all that we can with all that's known about HR practices and screening and recruiting people, and really using the professional body of knowledge that exists to screen out potential abusers as far as possible. No system will ever be perfect but ours is

pretty rigorous these days. We try to encourage a culture of disclosure of complaints.

Faith-based organizations often attract highly vulnerable members of the community, not only as service users but also as potential staff or volunteers who may be seeking to resolve their own issues through working with others (Smith 2006). Yet, at least in the past there was often resistance to subjecting staff or volunteers to rigorous scrutiny, on the basis that is wasn't needed in a religious setting. One of the Scottish research participants recalled a period a few years previously when she was on the board of management of the organization debating the need for police checking staff and volunteers:

> Fortunately we've not had anything but I know when I was on the board we were very concerned that our standards would be very high, that there was never the attitude around that would never happen to us because we're a Church. And it's interesting because in my own church life the issue around child protection and having child protection codes and training for within the Church who will be looking after children and various contacts I was around when that came in and tried to explain it to folk and they were saying but it did not happen to us because it's a Church. I said well actually we need to be very careful and because we're a Church, we probably need to be even more careful because – also because we're a Church we will attract folk who are very needy and who then think they can do other things and we need to be careful about what we put folk into, you know. And the one issue about even in the early days having to get full police checked and folks said 'why do I need that? I've never done anything' but you know we have to do it. So yes I think we would – it impacts on us I think in a way that we are very careful and the way we train our staff and also sometimes when you're working with child protection really you can focus so much on what the child discloses to you and what, for instance in our field of drug misuse, you know, what's happened to the child in their situation. But the other bit is about helping workers use safe practices and safe caring practices and how they manage how they are as workers as well.

The director of a small Australian faith-based organization described the procedure for checking potential volunteers as follows:

> We do five checks for volunteers before they get on to start work with us. So they have to go through an initial training and assessment programme and we're looking at not how great they're sort of coaching or their listening skills might be, but are they going to place the family at risk. Secondly, we do a reference check. Thirdly, we do a police

check. Fourthly, we do a working with children check and fifthly, we put them through a paedophile screening tool so that we are fairly confident. We're even actually looking at doing a psych test, but it just gets burdensome to actually employ a volunteer.

However, the need to implement such rigorous selection procedures may be resented. As the speaker in the previous quote went on to say:

But I suppose we're all victims in some sense that, you know, we're all having to now really be much more vigilant than we were because of a number of sex offenders in one or two Catholic churches and definitely we're being all tarred with the same brush.

One response of faith-based organizations to a troubled history is to become or appear more secular. In the main, many Scottish voluntary organizations which employ social workers have chosen to forgo their former religious identities in recent decades (Bondi 2013) whereas in Australia, some faith-based welfare organizations have considered their Christian identity to be problematic and have sought to remove obvious religious symbols from within the organization or to play down their religious identity (Swain 2005). For example, Wesley Central Mission in Melbourne adopted 'Social Role Valorization' as its guiding philosophy in the 1970s, arguing that it was congruent with Christian values, but presented a secular face to the world (Swain 2009).

While secularizing may result in services that are more appealing to some service users, there will remain others for whom welfare services which are steeped in their faith tradition will be what they desire and find most comforting (DeHart 2010). However, when service users present to a faith-based organization about issues of abuse which happened within the faith context, they may now be turned away if the agency believes there may be a conflict of interest between the service user and its auspice. For example, the manager of a service affiliated with one of the major Christian churches in Australia indicated that:

We've just had to be very careful if things around sexual abuse come in. Our policy would be if somebody was sexually abused by a church member we would not work with them . . . because one agency [organization] was sued because the person went . . . for counselling and they counselled them and then they felt that there was a conflict of interest.

Challenges for contemporary social work practice

Past practices which were abusive or problematic have not only required faith-based organizations to reconsider their practices, but they also present challenges for contemporary social work practice, particularly when service users have every right to be appalled at how they have been treated. A few research participants worked in organizations where allegations of abuse had been made and in some cases substantiated. Such allegations, even if they happened decades ago, may impact upon current staff. As one staff member explained:

> There's disclosures of abuse from this [organization]. . . . Whether people feel that they have been heard or haven't been heard. There's matters that have gone to the police that people have felt very confident that they would be successfully prosecuted in court but in fact they weren't. So there's a lot of legacy . . . and would certainly make people very, very cynical of any contact. And that's affected staff.

At other times service users are disaffected by other contact with the particular faith tradition rather than by the specific welfare organization through which contact is made. As a social worker in a very different organization to the previous speaker recalled:

> I had a family member I was working with, and there was one person, I think it was his uncle happened to be there one day and asked 'where are you from?' 'I'm from the Salvation Army' and he just went off. Now he apologized afterwards when I sat down with him and told him what my role is and what my experience of the Salvation Army is. . . . But that was enough to send him off the deep end a little bit. So you've got to be mindful. My first reaction was 'what's going on here?' and after he explained it and I sat down with him, he was able to say that was the reason why.

This particular social worker did not hold to the religious beliefs of their employer and it is possible that this enables a degree of detachment that makes it easier for social workers who are not members of the faith community associated with their employer to deal with service users who have been affected by past abuse. Conversely, social workers who strongly identify with the faith of their employer may have difficulties accepting that organizations where they work (or have worked) could be places where abuse of service users has occurred, and may vociferously deny that colleagues have been abusive despite evidence to the contrary (Smith 2008, 2010), and find it challenging when there is a need to provide service users with an opportunity to express their disdain or distrust of religious organizations or religious beliefs (Gilligan 2009).

Social workers in faith-based organizations may believe that their decisions and actions and those of their colleagues reflect the very high moral standards present in the religious teachings which underpin their agency (Chamiec-Case and Sherr 2006). Nevertheless, White (1997) cautions against a tendency among social workers to cling to naive viewpoints rather than wrestling with what are often much more complex and fraught realities. One way in which this may occur is to externalize the problem. In a city where the scandals concerned with sexual abuse were, at least in the public imagination, confined to the Catholic Church, a social worker in a non-Catholic faith-based organization may not consider the possibility of abusive practices being associated with their organization:

> Because scandals in [city] really came home, mostly around the local Catholic Church, so not sure what the response was in the community, in the organization, but I can imagine that people will take those situations and put them together with their perception of Christianity as a whole . . . because certainly there's no direct association between any particular Catholic churches with [organization]. If there had been scandals in say local Baptist or Pentecostal or Anglican churches, it might be more close to home and it might have more of an impact.

While it may well be that in this instance the previous speaker is correct in their assessment of the particular organization, there are sufficient well-publicized cases of sexual abuse in non-Catholic Christianity as well as in non-Christian religions to suggest that some doubt should be warranted (Crisp 2012). A strong emphasis on physical and sexual abuse may also lead to social workers not recognizing the many other ways in which their organizations may have engaged in practices once considered acceptable but which are now regarded as problematic (Smith 2008). In Australia in recent years, faith-based organizations have also been confronted with their now controversial historical roles in forcing single mothers to relinquish their babies for adoption and being complicit in government policies to remove indigenous children from their families and communities that has resulted in what is known as the 'Stolen Generation'. As a number of research participants noted, what was acceptable practice changes over time. For example:

> I think a lot of that occurs over time when our view of different practices evolves and we think back well how could have we approached that with an approach. But I think we've got to recall what was the context at the time and what did we understand, what were the values held at the time and so I do feel, I was going to say remorse and I was wondering if that was the right word, but I think that it is for instance around the missions and how we took Aboriginal children for instance away from their families into missions thinking that that was the best way to try and support them, but what we know now it isn't. So I do feel apologetic for the way we've practised in the past, but at the same time feel that our forebears were doing what they thought was the best thing.

In light of such experiences, social workers may come to realize that in the future they too may find themselves confronted by the viewpoint that the ways in which they practise have been discredited. However, organizations that are able to confront past wrongs and evolve not only have the capacity to achieve longevity, but also provide the working conditions in which individual social workers can mature in their practice. As one social worker commented:

> I think one of the reference points in our day-to-day practice is – how is this going to be viewed in 10 years' time or 20 years' time in that what people did, whether it be 20 years ago or 50 years ago, they thought they were doing the right thing at that time. I would also want to acknowledge that whatever they were doing, and within the faith-based agency, this state is also doing if possible, or they had asked the Church to do it and I think to the credit of, well in particular I would say this in relation to Christian agencies because this is what I would be more familiar with, they stood the test of time. They have been harshly judged and perceived and judged and rightly so, but they continued to stand the test of time, acknowledging their shortfalls within all that. There were enormous shortfalls and things that you would feel deeply pained about or ashamed about but in another way, I think it is something about a faith-based agency not being dependent on an individual. It is dependent on principles and values well beyond the individual and that is what the gospel is about. I think we are easy to target. I think we are making a statement that it is right that we get challenged, but I think we are much easier to target as well because we stand there proclaiming a professional base and sadly we don't always meet up to it, but we are human too.

Importantly, service users are human too and need to be considered as holistic beings. As Smith (2006) has rightly commented in respect of residential childcare, regulation may lead to less overt abuse in the future, but rigid no-touch rules, resulting in a child never receiving what are generally regarded as normal and acceptable signs of affection, can lead to the dehumanization of both those in care and their carers (Smith 2006).

For social workers in faith-based organizations, the historical controversies, either in their own organization or of the sector more generally, may also present challenges in their dealings with other organizations. As one Australian social worker commented in respect of sexual abuse, 'It certainly has had an impact and it certainly has had an impact on our relationships with the advocacy services for forgotten Australians who would think that everyone who grew up in a Catholic home must have been abused.'

Conclusion

As this chapter has demonstrated, being a faith-based organization does not ensure good or appropriate social work practice and in fact strongly religious teachings have at times enabled poor or abusive practices to be overshadowed (Green 2010). Furthermore, an actual or perceived history of controversial practices can have consequences today for organizations and their staff, particularly when working with service users who have experienced abuse while under the care of a faith-based organization.

Although many of the research participants were aware of their organization having shameful aspects of its history, this applied more to participants in organizations which at some point in their history have been providers of residential services, particularly to children. However, even if their treatment of service users has not involved the level of abuse outlined by some organizations in this chapter, what is regarded as best practice now may well be discredited at some point in the future (Brennan-Krohn 2011). At a much more subtle level social work in many settings, including faith-based organizations, has upheld rather than challenged inequalities, and has opened up the profession to the charge that:

> Social work long ago diminished itself from a social cause to an institutional function. . . . Ours, despite the efforts of many, can be a profession that reproduces inequalities, reinforces the norms of the market state, and uses therapy as a way of helping people to feel better about the social justices in their lives.
>
> (Graham *et al.* 2011: 189–190)

It may be argued that to some degree, faith-based organizations should not necessarily take all the blame for abusive practices and that the state has often been complicit. States have often colluded with poor care practices by furnishing minimal or insufficient funds to religious groups to care for children (Murray *et al.* 2009) and failing to set standards of care. Furthermore, rather than establishing inspection regimes which examined whether suitable care was being provided, states were often willing to trust that faith-based organizations would be providing adequate care (Swain 2009). Moreover, the state was not just lax in supervising care regimes in the faith-based sector but, in Australia at least, there is also evidence that abuse of children was also occurring in institutions run by the state and other non-government groups (Senate Community Affairs Reference Committee 2004).

While all welfare organizations should be able to stand up to public scrutiny, at times it appears that faith-based organizations have been singled out to take the blame for abuse which occurred not just within but also beyond the sector. In addition to identifying faults where they occur, critical scrutiny of faith-based organizations also needs to recognize any good work that is being done (Scales 2011). The most recent revisions of the *Code of Ethics* of the Australian Association of Social Workers (AASW) reminds social workers that, irrespective of their own religious beliefs, ethical social work practice includes providing due respect to faith-based organizations:

> Social workers will recognise, acknowledge and remain sensitive to and respectful of the religious and spiritual world views of individuals, groups, communities and social networks, and the operations and missions of faith and spiritually-based organisations.
>
> (AASW 2010: 18)

Clearly, histories of controversy can present challenges for contemporary faith-based organizations and the social workers employed in such organizations. Chapter 8 further considers challenges for faith-based organizations.

8

CHALLENGES AND OPPORTUNITIES

Public faith . . . engages with service delivery, with community cohesion and in governance. In each of these arenas it encounters, and is encountered by, a whole range of differing values, goals, practices and languages. The challenge is to respond in a context of mutuality, reciprocity and trust if the shared meal at the public table is not to result in indigestion.

(Dinham 2009: 204)

Introduction

As Adam Dinham suggests in the above quotation, faith-based organizations frequently find themselves at intersections which must be negotiated if they are to advance into the future with integrity. Historical notions of what it meant to be a faith-based organization have been placed under scrutiny in some organizations with questions raised as to what it means now to be faith-based. Faith communities may no longer desire or be in a position to support long-standing programmes or initiatives and may themselves be struggling to remain in existence. Governments and other funding bodies may consider faith-based organizations favourably, particularly if they regard them as a lower cost solution to providing for the welfare of individuals and communities. However, others may view them with suspicion and even argue that in increasingly secular communities, faith-based organizations are an anachronism. In addition, there are questions about religious beliefs and what role, if any, they have in both the running of a welfare organization and the programmes that are offered by a faith-based organization. This chapter further considers some of these challenges as well as opportunities for faith-based organizations.

Challenges

Previous chapters have identified many challenges which faith-based organizations may encounter. Many of these challenges may be clustered into concerns about identity, organizational arrangements and funding. Each will be discussed in turn.

Identity

The identity of faith-based organizations can create challenges from a number of perspectives both within faith-based organizations and in their interactions with the wider communities in which they work. Although sometimes regarded by the wider world as if homogeneous, such generalizations are problematic, and faith-based organizations may find assumptions being made about them which are far from their specific reality. There is a wide diversity of faith-based organizations with differing sizes, structures, histories, missions and ways of working. Furthermore, religious and secular discourses can be so similar as to not be distinctive (Sosin and Smith 2006), resulting in faith-based organizations sometimes appearing to be more similar to their secular counterparts than to some other faith-based organizations (Ferris 2011; Thaut 2009). In particular, meeting regulatory requirements may take precedence over working in accordance with religious beliefs or teaching (Sosin and Smith 2006) and, as a manager in a Scottish faith-based organization explained:

> I suppose, that is one of the challenges and I think the other thing is, I suppose the challenge for faith-based agencies and churches is how do you make that link, how do you make that link between what makes a faith-based agency different from an ordinary [field of practice] agency? What is different about us, and that's quite a challenge in a sense, because we use the same paperwork that everybody else uses, we follow the same . . . process that other agencies do.

In such situations, the distinctiveness of faith-based organizations can be lost. An Australian social worker, while believing that his own organization was still maintaining its faith-based identity despite receiving significant government funding, recognized this potential, and had observed it occurring in other faith-based organizations:

> My one fear for it would be that it would lose its spirit, its ethos. I don't think it has, I think it's kept it, but I'm not sure what it needs to do to in order to make sure it does keep it. I know places that have lost it . . . I've talked to people in other places, they say, 'oh it's just changed since this has happened'. They get really down about losing that spirit.

While there may be good reasons why a faith-based organization does not display an explicitly religious identity in its dealings with the wider community, the question remains as to whether an organization understands what having a faith basis means (Thaut 2009), particularly if that faith basis was closely bound up with particular individuals. As many faith-based organizations have found, once links with the founders are no longer present, maintaining the initial vision, or aspects of it that are still relevant can become an ongoing challenge (Holden and Trembath 2008; Lake 2013). For example, social workers employed in some Catholic welfare organizations talked about the decreasing involvement of the vowed religious who historically played a major role in running the services. An Australian social worker expressed her concerns as follows:

> I guess that, probably my hope would be, that there would always be something in this organization that would hold it very true to our founding spirit, and that there would be enough keepers of the spirit in the organization that could influence the people who come to work here. . . . Some of the faith-based organizations have much less of a connection to the church than others do, and ours will be challenging because the religious congregations are diminishing, they're ageing.

Retaining a religious identity can be facilitated by having key staff who have a good appreciation of the founding vision which established the organization and able to build on that mission (Bielefeld and Cleveland 2013). As the Catholic director of an Australian Catholic welfare agency explained:

> When I first came into the network and I think this is modelled say in Catholic education, most of the directors were religious or ex-religious so they had a background in faith or church or whatever. Now those people are leaving, the same in principals in schools now, so how do you get I suppose that . . . I don't think it's being a good Catholic, I might not be classed as a good Catholic, but it's how do you get an understanding of the values, the ethos of where something came from?

It is not just an issue for Catholic agencies. The capacity of faith-based organizations from many faith traditions to expand their work and maintain a distinctive faith-based agenda or focus should not be assumed (Belcher and Tice 2011), particularly in an era when many faith-based agencies are already employing substantial numbers of staff from outside their faith bases, some of whom may have no religious beliefs at all. Nevertheless, some faith-based organizations do manage to retain their faith identity, despite diminishing numbers of staff who are of the faith, but this requires intentional effort from the organization, and may disappear if left to chance.

The faith basis of an organization may also be obscured by partnership arrangements with other organizations who may not recognize or acknowledge the faith basis of their partners (Dinham 2009). As one Scottish social worker commented, such arrangements may be a financial necessity but present challenges for faith-based organizations in respect of their identity:

> The big challenge is . . . we need to work in partnership with other agencies. Can we maintain our distinctiveness in that in the future? Not too worried about that in the immediate future but I think later on that might be an issue. In the end it's all down to money, you know, the Church is not overflowing with money.

Some faith-based agencies which have distanced themselves publicly from their religious roots have in recent years been making their religious links more explicit (Holden and Trembath 2008). Indeed, if they wish to continue to identify as faith based, articulating one's faith basis is essential. The British author Helen Cameron has proposed three questions which she believes any organization identifying as Christian should be able to answer. These are as follows:

1   What do you believe about the relationship between divine agency and human agency?
2   What do you believe about the relationship between beliefs and actions?
3   What do you believe about human well-being?

(Cameron 2004: 147)

Although framed within the context of Christianity, to varying degrees, her questions, particularly the latter two, may well be asked of faith-based organizations of any religion. Moreover, as Cameron explains, even Christian organizations may answer these questions in very different ways, reflecting their theological emphases and rationales for service delivery. Cameron notes how a service such as a food pantry can be provided for very different reasons and reflect very different theologies.

While there may be other questions which it would be more salient than those which Cameron (2004) proposes should be asked of faith-based organizations, organizations that cannot articulate their faith basis, and how it influences how they work, are likely to struggle to maintain a faith-based identity. Ultimately, some organizations may find they need to address the question as to whether they really are a faith-based organization and if their vision is of them being faith based. While casting off a faith identity may have benefits for an organization in removing challenges associated with religious beliefs, organizations should also consider what benefits might accrue by remaining a faith-based organization and whether forgoing these benefits is an acceptable price for a faith-less identity. On the other hand, as the director of a Scottish faith-based organization noted, there may also be substantial challenges for faith-based organizations which choose to retain a faith identity in societies where religion no longer has the level of community respect that it may have generated in the past:

> For faith-based organizations, I think the big challenge has been already in a way forced upon us, which is a kind of increasingly secularized sort of society and a diminishing role of religion and faith in public life and I think that's been ongoing for quite a number of years now and I think as voluntary agencies, with faith-based, we've had to kind of manage that and deal with that, because I think it's hard to stand up in witness to your faith in a very public way now in particular. And it was always quite hard in a social work setting I think, but actually it's becoming more so, because I think the sort of accepted respect for religion and its part in society to a large extent's gone. There's no longer assumptions about, well why should a church have special dispensation for one thing or another; whether it's tax, benefits; all those things. I think that sort of sense of the importance of faith is a big challenge in society and in our work and for us to be able to hold onto that.

Organizational arrangements

Faith-based organizations not only need a vision of what it means to be faith-based, but also the acumen to put this into practice. As an Australian social worker spoke of his former faith-based employer:

> Certainly for [organization], they've got to understand what they really mean, what they want to do with social work, in relation to their spiritual side of things. I think there's a perfect fit, but they just don't get it. They could do it very differently, still do it well, but do it very differently and I expect provide improved outcomes for clients. But I think also that part of that is they need to change with the times. I'm not just talking around beliefs. That's – I'm not suggesting they should change their beliefs, but the way they practise.

Maintaining relevance requires organizations to have a vision as to what they could achieve in the future and not assume that what has been done in the past is necessarily appropriate in the future. In other words, faith-based organizations need to be able to respond to changing needs and circumstances, and have leadership which sees this as critical rather than being committed to maintaining a status quo (Lake 2013). As the speaker in the previous quote went on to talk about members of the religious hierarchy who oversaw the faith-based organization where he had worked:

> One of the issues . . . for instance, was they weren't growing. One of my bosses actually said they were quite happy not to grow, which if you're not growing, you're dying basically. So I think there's real issues in that for them. They lack vision for their social work arm and it shouldn't be an arm, it should be all together.

Historically, a frequent critique of faith-based organizations is that prioritizing employment of people of faith often resulted in skill shortages. Although there are some religious leaders who also have social work degrees or other human service qualifications, and many others do take seriously the recommendations of their social work and welfare qualified staff, for faith-based organizations in which the ultimate decision-making body is religious leaders it leaves open the potential for anachronistic decision-making. While it may be argued that such organizational structures ensure organizations retain their faith identities, this should not be at the expense of being able to develop organizational vision which is both forward thinking and reflecting a deep understanding of the social and political context within which the organization seeks to work (Dinham 2012a). But even if faith-based organizations are not particularly visionary, maintaining dual accountabilities to secular and religious authorities is a continual challenge (Vanderwoerd 2004), as is being responsive, operating professionally and effectively performing key tasks (Harb 2008).

Effective organizational arrangements are not just essential for individual faith-based organizations but also for working in partnerships with other organizations, whether faith based or not. Kidwai and Haider (2007) have suggested that faith-based organizations entering into partnerships should at a minimum have shared concerns, agreement as to how to address these concerns and agreed processes for evaluating the work. In order to sustain partnerships, each organization also needs organizational structures which facilitate working with other organizations and the ability to foster 'goodwill' with partners.

In any partnership situation, the question of who can speak on behalf of the partnership should be negotiated once the partnership is established. With faith-based organizations this may be particularly important, as it may not be considered reasonable to expect one individual or organization to speak on behalf of diverse faith perspectives (Chapman and Lowndes 2009). Senior staff of individual faith-based organizations may be empowered to speak publicly on issues but there may be expectations that on some issues public comment is made by religious officials. Conversely, so-called 'faith representatives' or 'leaders' are not necessarily authorized to speak on behalf of the members or organizations associated with particular religions or accountable to them (Dinham and Lowndes 2008).

Most of the above suggestions about organizational arrangements are not particular to faith-based organizations, and may apply as good advice to anyone seeking to establish a welfare organization employing professional staff. Furthermore, the organizational structures of some religions are highly bureaucratic and individuals within those religious traditions seeking to establish a new faith-based initiative may well expect to be able to articulate a wide range of organizational processes even before a new organization is established. However, some faith-based welfare initiatives have emerged as a good idea and have attracted goodwill but have lacked sustainable organizational structures to support them, and hence it should not be assumed that new faith-based organizations necessarily have appropriate organizational structures to take on certain initiatives. Similarly, existing faith-based organizations may have organizational structures which may serve the needs of some stakeholders, such as their religious hierarchies, but not necessarily be appropriate for running a contemporary welfare organization or alternately enable the running of a welfare programme but disenfranchising the religious auspice. In addition, as the external demands continue to change, ensuring appropriate organizational structures is likely to be an ongoing challenge for many faith-based organizations.

Funding

Funding is an ongoing challenge for many faith-based organizations. Long-established organizations which may once have been supported by their religious communities may no longer be able to rely on such support. As a research participant who had worked with Jewish organizations noted, when donating money to charitable causes, many community members were no longer prioritizing Jewish organizations:

> The other problem that all Jewish organizations around in the developed world were facing is that younger Jewish people were more likely to give their money to a cause that they were passionate about which may be Jewish but it could also be green energy, it could be refugees. So Jewish organizations have typically depended on the loyalty of the Jewish community and that is a question for the future about whether Jewish younger people will want to give their money to a Jewish organization or [to somewhere else].

However, it is not just Jewish organizations that are facing the challenge of diminishing contributions from their community. In respect of Christian organizations, active membership of churches is declining, which may require them to seek charitable funds from beyond their membership, as another research participant suggested:

> I think a lot of faith-based agencies have had considerable independent funding from congregations who support them and in the future that's not going to be the case at all. So it's finding alternative means of fundraising, whether that's through *philanthropic* trusts or the bequests and things like that.

Faith-based organizations which apply for philanthropic funding may well be competing for limited funds with a wide range of other community groups, and find that their faith basis does not advantage them, and perhaps even disadvantages them if the trustees consider that faith-based groups have more access to social and other forms of capital than do other community groups. Furthermore, much philanthropic funding is often time limited and insufficient to pay the full-time salary costs of professional staff such as social workers, so it is not necessarily a long-term funding solution.

For faith-based organizations which grow to a level larger than can be supported by their religious community, state funding is often the only viable source of ongoing funds. This often requires faith-based organizations to reframe their visions and methods of working in order to fit within bureaucratic guidelines, and ultimately can have detrimental effects upon the organization (Baker 2009). Consequently, questions can emerge concerning how pragmatic faith-based organizations should be as they seek to balance their resources, the needs of service users, legislative and societal expectations with their own beliefs and ideologies (Sosin and Smith 2006). A Scottish social worker expressed this dilemma as follows:

> I think, the trouble with, the biggest challenge at the moment is financial and very often we as an organization are being expected to reduce our faith-based part of our organization not to be so God like ... I always think that we are diverting our faith because, I feel, I won't usually believe that, that I think that 'We'll just not bother about that because if we go that way we'll not get the money, but if we drop our beliefs we're more likely to get the money from the local authority'.

Funding organizations tend to be inclined to invest in organizations or programmes which use funds efficiently. In the words of another Scottish social worker:

> Like other organizations in [City], they have to compete for funding as a service, so they have to be able to convince the local authority that they are value for money and that they provide value for money and that they're providing a valuable service.

Because they are often known to have resources of their own which they contribute to the running of programmes, faith-based organizations can be an attractive option for funders who are seeking to stretch their limited resources as far as possible. However, it is important that faith-based organizations should not feel they are being forced into subsidizing the state when running programmes on its behalf. Faith-based organizations should feel that their contributions to the well-being of the wider community are valued and worthwhile, and it needs to be recognized that for faith-based organizations:

> The positive risk to their investment is that they increase their influence, acquire greater networks and secure actual hard economic capital as well. Conversely, the negative risk is that they may become disoriented and burnt out in meeting the extra demands put on them.
>
> (Baker 2009: 114)

Inadequate funding means that social workers in faith-based organizations are often paid less than their counterparts working for the state. While many faith-based organizations are still attractive employers despite staff salaries, relying on the goodwill of social workers who are prepared to work for less than if they worked for the state may eventually compromise the quality of staff members who they are able to recruit and retain and consequently the quality of service which is delivered.

Opportunities

Despite some considerable challenges which faith-based organizations may face, there may also be many opportunities afforded by the social and policy contexts in which faith-based organizations are situated and through having some resources which are not dependent upon outside funding. Perhaps even more importantly, the strong values base which underpins many faith-based organizations can influence both policy decisions and shape social work practice.

Social and policy context

Although the state plays a dominant role in setting the policy context in which faith-based organizations operate, states are often reliant on faith-based organizations to deliver a range of services to individuals and communities in need (Murphy 2007). Faith-based organizations, especially those which have strong links with their religious communities, may be able to reach and engage with segments of the community, particularly marginalized communities, with which state instrumentalities struggle to connect. Despite the claims of some that religion is on the decline and secularism is on the ascendant,

> Religious faith has nevertheless remained a hugely significant social phenomenon and has come to be dominated by social policy perspectives which see faith groups as rich in resources which can be put to general use. By happy coincidence, it is hoped, they will lend their keenness on and talent for 'community' to wider society. They will field their many volunteers to welfare projects and services. Even minority faith groups can be enlisted to the mainstream of society, bringing their cultural baggage with them and thereby averting the risk of radicalization which can otherwise take place at the margins; and where a minority of fundamentalists are drawn into violent extremism there are policies at hand to work with 'good' faith groups to reach out to the 'bad'.
>
> (Dinham 2012a: 9–10)

While faith-based organizations may well find themselves co-opted by the state which is seeking to develop community cohesion and build social capital (Ager and Ager 2011), partnership arrangements may provide opportunities for faith-based organizations to contribute new perspectives to policy debates (Dinham 2009; Jennings and Clarke 2008).

Social work practice

Often regarded as a strength of many faith-based agencies is practice which is underpinned by a strong values basis. While values-based practice can occur in a wide range of settings, faith-based organizations have the potential to model how this can occur (Fulford and Woodbridge 2007), especially when they 'insist on questions which have fallen out of fashion, about what it is to be human, how to interact as well as transact, the source and character of human value, the role of love, and yes, the meaning of life' (Dinham 2009: 208–209).

At its most basic level, a strong values base is evident in many faith-based organizations when the dignity of human life is not an optional extra (Ranson 2012). As Dinham has noted:

> [D]ignity in religious terms, resides in human *being*, not human enterprise. According to faith traditions, it is human difference and variety which makes life interesting and valuable, and emphasizing markets over people, rather than people in markets, sets parameters which narrow the terms of celebration of the human life.
>
> (Dinham 2012a: 94–95)

In social work practice, this may be evident in approaches where service users are treated 'as persons, not simply as cases' (Lake 2013: 218) and where basic hospitality is integral to the provision of care rather than a needless expense (Ranson 2012). As previously argued, faith-based organizations:

> have and can continue to make a distinct contribution to social welfare provision . . . by offering models of service delivery which have sought not to excise the spiritual from the more prosaic needs with which individuals present when seeking assistance from welfare providers. However, for this to be most effective, a whole of agency approach is required rather than leaving consideration of matters spiritual to those staff involved in direct service delivery.
>
> (Crisp 2010: 451)

A whole of agency approach to forms of service delivery which takes account of the spiritual needs of service users includes the value basis which underpins strategic decision-making within a faith-based organization. A strong values base may lead to faith-based organizations taking a prophetic stance, particularly by working in solidarity with vulnerable and marginalized groups (Horstmann 2011; Parsitau 2011). Faith-based organizations have long been innovators, often developing new services which are later taken up by the state (Lake 2013), and it may be argued that being able to take a prophetic stance facilitates longevity. Long-term survival for faith-based organizations may be more likely among those which have an advocacy component, which can identify new needs and adapt to provide those services, rather than only being able to deliver existing services (Kaseman and Austin 2005). This is particularly so if proposals for new services are underpinned by a vision that is consistent with the organization's vision (Lake 2013).

A further possible contribution of faith-based organizations to social work practice concerns skill development in respect of service users who present to social workers with concerns in which religion or spirituality is potentially an issue. Sheridan *et al.* (1992) have suggested that as many as one-third of all US service users present with such issues and recently it has been proposed that 'it is a social work task to understand, consider and develop religious literacy to work effectively with vulnerable people' (Melville-Wiseman 2013: 300). Yet many social workers, particularly in secular agencies, practise in ways which ignore the religious dimension of service users (Furness and Gilligan 2010a). While this can reflect a fear that any mention of religion may be construed by service users as a form of proselytizing, many faith-based organizations have developed skills in working sensitively with service users from a wide range of faiths and of no faith, which could be adapted to non-faith-based settings.

Conclusion

This book has argued that there can be a legitimate place for faith-based welfare organizations, and a legitimate role for professional social workers within such organizations. However, such claims are not uncontested and faith-based organizations may need to work hard to develop policies and processes which will result in being considered credible by a wide range of stakeholders, including service users, staff, funders and the wider community.

The relationship between religion and social work 'is long-standing, dense, complicated, contested, and ever-evolving, all the way up to the present day' (Scales and Kelly 2011: 356), and hence the roles and activities of faith-based organizations in welfare provision have never been static and are unlikely to become so (Furness and Gilligan 2012). This book has focused on some situations in which the involvement of faith-based organizations has been controversial, if not fraught, but has also identified areas where the scope for involvement of faith-based organizations has not been fully realized.

As the potential scope for faith-based organizations is expanding in many countries where participation in formal religion is decreasing (Crisp 2013), it may well be that religion is not disappearing but changing its form and expression such that it is much more likely than in the past to be manifested in forms of welfare provision (Bäckström *et al.* 2011). While this volume has begun to address the lack of research about social work in faith-based organizations outside the US, and in particular has provided perspectives from countries such as Australia and Scotland where previous research in this area has been limited, perhaps more questions have been raised than have been answered. Clearly further research is needed and it is hoped that some of the issues raised in this book will lead to further research in other countries, or about social work in faith-based organizations associated with particular religions.

Yet even without further research, this book argues that those of us who work in or whose work requires us to engage with faith-based organizations may well need a much more sophisticated understanding of the range of faith-based organizations than is often held either by social workers or the wider community. Not only is this grouping not homogeneous, but the potential scope for social work practice and for practice dilemmas arising from this work will vary considerably depending on the national and religious context. While this book has endeavoured to identify a range of positions where variations exist, there may well be even further alternatives not identified in the research undertaken to inform the writing of this book.

As a grouping, faith-based organizations are full of surprises, often defy simplistic assumptions and may well stand up to scrutiny from their staunchest critics. Conversely, their staunchest supporters may need to recognize that faith-based organizations can be deeply flawed and have been found to be unethical in their practice. If this book has done no more than encouraged readers to move beyond their stereotypes of faith-based organizations, then some of the aims of this project will have been realized.

REFERENCES

AASW (2010) *Code of Ethics*, Canberra: Australian Association of Social Workers. Online. Available: http://www.aasw.asn.au/document/item/740 (accessed 14 June 2013).

Ager, A. and Ager, J. (2011) 'Faith and the discourse of secular humanism', *Journal of Refugee Studies*, 24(3): 456–472.

Ahmed, M., Cantle, T. and Hussain, D. (2009) 'Faith, multiculturalism and community cohesion: a policy conversation', in A. Dinham, R. Furbey and V. Lowndes (eds) *Faith in the Public Realm: Controversies, policies and practices*, Bristol: The Policy Press.

Alcock, P. (1997) *Understanding Poverty*, 2nd edn, Basingstoke: Macmillan.

Alison, J. (2010) *Broken Hearts and New Creations: Intimations of a great reversal*, London: Darton, Longman & Todd.

Al-Krenawi, A. and Graham, J.R. (2008) 'Localizing social work with Bedouin-Arab communities in Israel: limitations and possibilities', in M. Gray, J. Coates and M. Yellowbird (eds) *Indigenous Social Work Around the World: Towards culturally relevant practice*, Aldershot: Ashgate.

Andersen, J.A. (2004) 'Vicars vs. managers: do vicars differ from managers in terms of leadership behaviour?', *Journal of Management, Spirituality and Religion*, 1(2): 201–223.

Angell, O.H. (2010) 'Sacred welfare agents in secular welfare space: the Church of Norway in Drammen', in A. Bäckström, G. Davie, N. Edgardh and P. Pettersson (eds) *Welfare and Religion in 21st Century Europe: Volume 1 Configuring the connections*, Farnham: Ashgate.

Angell, O.H. and Wyller, T. (2006) 'The Church of Norway as an agent of welfare: the case of Drammen', in A.B. Yeung, N. Edgardh Beckman and P. Pettersson (eds) *Churches in Europe as Agents of Welfare: Sweden, Norway and Finland*, Uppsala: Institute for Diaconal and Social Studies.

Ashencaen Crabtree, S., Hussain, F. and Spalek, B. (2008) *Islam and Social Work: Debating values, transforming practice*, Bristol: The Policy Press.

Ashford, S. and Timms, N. (1990) 'Values in social work: investigations of the practice of family placement', *British Journal of Social Work*, 29(1): 1–20.

Austin, M. (2003) 'The changing relationship between nonprofit organizations and public social service agencies in the era of welfare reform', *Nonprofit and Voluntary Sector Quarterly*, 32(1): 97–114.

Ayton, D., Carey, G., Keleher, H. and Smith, B. (2012) 'Historical overview of church involvement in health and wellbeing in Australia: implications for health promotion partnerships', *Australian Journal of Primary Health*, 18(1): 4–10.

Bäckström, A. and Davie, G. (2010) 'The WREP Project: genesis, structure and scope', in A. Bäckström, G. Davie, N. Ergardh and P. Pettersson (eds) *Welfare and Religion in 21st Century Europe: Volume 1 Configuring the connections*, Farnham: Ashgate.

Bäckström, A., Davie, G., Ergardh, N. and Pettersson, P. (eds) (2010) *Welfare and Religion in 21st Century Europe: Volume 1 Configuring the connections*, Farnham: Ashgate.

Bäckström, A., Davie, G., Edgardh, N. and Pettersson, P. (2011) 'The WREP Project: building bridges', in A. Bäckström, G. Davie, N. Edgardh and P. Pettersson (eds) *Welfare and Religion in 21st Century Europe: Volume 2 Gendered religious and social change*, Farnham: Ashgate.

Bacon, D. (2011) 'Faith-based organisations and welfare provision in Northern Ireland and North America: whose agenda?', in C. Milligan and D. Conradson (eds) *Landscapes of Voluntarism: New spaces of health, welfare and governance*, Bristol: The Policy Press.

Baker, C. (2009) 'Blurred encounters? Religious literacy, spiritual capital and language', in A. Dinham, R. Furbey and V. Lowndes (eds) *Faith in the Public Realm: Controversies, policies and practices*, Bristol: The Policy Press.

Baker, C. (2012) 'Spiritual capital and economies of grace: redefining the relationship between religion and the welfare state', *Social Policy and Society*, 11(4): 565–576.

Barbosa da Silva, A. (2009) 'How Christian norms can have an impact on bioethics in a pluralist and democratic Europe: a Scandinavian perspective', *Christian Bioethics*, 15(1): 54–73.

Barise, A. (2005) 'Social work with Muslims: insights from the teaching of Islam', *Critical Social Work*, 6(2). Online. Available at www1.uwindsor.ca/critical socialwork/social-work-with-muslims-insights-from-the-teachings-of-Islam (accessed 7 October 2013).

Barnardos (2013) *Research and Lobbying Government*. Online. Available: http://www.barnardos.org.uk/what_we_do/policy_research_unit.htm (accessed 9 June 2013).

Battin, M.P. (1990) *Ethics in the Sanctuary: Examining the practices of organized religion*, New Haven, CT: Yale University Press.

Belcher, H. (2008) 'Explaining a paradox: church and health policy in the 1940s and 1970s', *Australasian Catholic Record*, 85(3): 259–273.

Belcher, J.R. and DeForge, B.R. (2007) 'Faith-based social services: the challenges of providing assistance', *Journal of Religion and Spirituality in Social Work*, 26(4): 1–19.

Belcher, J.R. and Tice, C.J. (2011) 'Protestant church charity: history, trends and implications', *Journal of Religion and Spirituality in Social Work*, 30(2): 164–177.

Benedetti, C. (2006) 'Islamic and Christian inspired relief NGOs: between tactical collaboration and tactical diffidence?', *Journal of International Development*, 18(6): 849–859.

Benedict XVI (2006) *Deus Caritas Est.* Online. Available: http://www.vatican.va/holy_father/benedict_xvi/encyclicals/documents/hf_ben-xvi_enc_20051225_deus-caritas-est_en.html (accessed 29 July 2012).

Benthall, J. (2007) 'Muslim NGOs: the overreaction against Islamic charities', *Isim Review*, 20: 6–7.

Berger, J. (2003) 'Religious non-governmental organizations: an exploratory analysis', *Voluntas* 14(1): 15–39.

Bielefeld, W. and Cleveland, W.S. (2013) 'Defining faith-based organizations and understanding them through research', *Nonprofit and Voluntary Sector Quarterly*, 42(3): 442–467.

Boddie, S.C. and Cnaan, R.A. (2006) *Faith-based Social Services: Measures, assessments, and effectiveness*, Binghamton, NY: Haworth Pastoral Press.

Boddie, S.C., Hong, P.J.P., Im, H. and Chung, S. (2011) 'Korean-American churches as partners in community development', *Social Work and Christianity*, 38(4): 395–416.

Bondi, L. (2011) 'The changing landscape of voluntary sector counselling in Scotland', in C. Milligan and D. Conradson (eds) *Landscapes of Voluntarism: New spaces of health, welfare and governance*, Bristol: The Policy Press.

Bondi, L. (2013) 'Between Christianity and secularity: counselling and psychotherapy provision in Scotland', *Social and Cultural Geography*, 14(6): 668–688.

Bowpitt, G. (1998) 'Evangelical Christianity, secular humanism and the genesis of British social work', *British Journal of Social Work*, 28(5): 675–693.

Brauns, H-J. and Kramer, D. (1995) 'Germany', in T.D. Watts, D. Elliott and N.S. Mayadas (eds) *International Handbook on Social Work Education*, Wesport, CT: Greenwood Press.

Brenden, M.A. (2007) 'Social work for social justice: strengthening social work practice through the integration of Catholic Social Teaching', *Social Work and Christianity*, 34(4): 472–497.

Brennan-Krohn, Z. (2011) 'Negotiating the twentieth century: a historical analysis of Camphill communities', in R. Jackson (ed.) *Discovering Camphill: New perspectives, research and developments*, Edinburgh: Floris Books.

Briggs, S., Whittacker, A., Linford, H., Bryan, A., Ryan, E. and Ludick, D. (2011) *Safeguarding Children's Rights: Exploring issues of witchcraft and spirit possession in London's African communities*, London: Trust for London. Online. Available: http://www.trustforlondon.org.uk/Safeguarding%20final%20report.pdf (accessed 1 July 2013).

BSL (2012) *Annual Report 2012*, Fitzroy, Victoria: Brotherhood of St Laurence. Online. Available: http://www.bsl.org.au/pdfs/BSL_2012_AR_WEB.pdf (accessed 22 May 2013).

BSL (2013) *About the Brotherhood*. Online. Available: http://www.bsl.org.au/About-the-Brotherhood (accessed 22 May 2013).

Cameron, H. (2004) 'Typology of religious characteristics of social service and educational organizations and programs: a European response', *Nonprofit and Voluntary Sector Quarterly*, 33(1): 146–150.

Camilleri, P. and Winkworth, G. (2004) 'Mapping the Catholic social services', *The Australasian Catholic Record*, 81(2): 184–197.

Camilleri, P. and Winkworth, G. (2005) 'Catholic Social Services in Australia: a short history', *Australian Social Work*, 58(1): 76–85.

Campbell, F. (2009) 'New development: faith and foreign policy – a perspective from the Vatican', *Public Money and Management*, 29(6): 347–350.

Campbell, S. (2012) 'Explosion of the Spirit: a spiritual journey into the 2010 Healthcare Reform Legislation', *Journal of Religion and Spirituality in Social Work*, 31(1–2): 85–104.

Caritas Care (2013a) *Who Can Adopt?* Online. Available: http://www.caritascare.org.uk/adoption-fostering/adoption/who-can-adopt/ (accessed 26 June 2013).

Caritas Care (2013b) *Statement of Values*. Online. Available: http://www.caritascare.org.uk/about/statement-of-values/ (accessed 26 June 2013).

Cascio, T. (2003) 'Religious foundations of charity', in T. Tirrito and T. Cascio (eds) *Religious Organizations in Community Services: A social work perspective*, New York: Springer Publishing.

Castles, F.G. (2002) 'Australia's institutions and Australia's welfare state', in G. Brennan and F. Castles (eds) *Australia Reshaped: 200 years of institutional transformation*, Melbourne: Cambridge University Press.

Catholic Social Services Victoria (2013) *Current Members*. Online.: http://www.css.org.au/Members/Current-Members.aspx (accessed 15 March 2013).

Cemlyn, S. and Briskman, L. (2003) 'Asylum, children's rights and social work', *Child and Family Social Work*, 8(3): 163–178.

Challen, M.B. (1996) 'The changing roles of church and state in Australian welfare provision', *Social Security Journal*, June: 26–31.

Chambre, S.M. (2001) 'The changing nature of "faith" in faith-based organizations: secularization and ecumenicism in four AIDS organizations in New York City', *Social Service Review*, 75(3): 435–455.

Chamiec-Case, R. and Sherr, M. (2006) 'Exploring how social work administrators integrate spirituality in the workplace', *Social Work and Christianity*, 33(3): 268–287.

Chapman, R. (2009) 'Faith and the voluntary sector in urban governance: distinctive yet similar?', in A. Dinham, R. Furbey and V. Lowndes (eds) *Faith in the Public Realm: Controversies, policies and practices*, Bristol: The Policy Press.

Chapman, R. and Lowndes, V. (2009) 'Accountable, authorized or authentic? What do "faith representatives" offer urban governance?', *Public Money and Management*, 29(6): 371–378.

Charities Aid Foundation (2013) *The Search Tool*. Online. Available: http://www.charitytrends.org/SearchTool_Step1.aspx (accessed 30 June 2013).

Charnley, H. (2007) 'Reflections on the role and performance of international organizations in supporting children separated from their families by war', *Ethics and Social Welfare*, 1(3): 253–268.

Cheit, R.E., Shavit, Y. and Reiss-Davis, Z. (2010) 'Magazine coverage of child sexual abuse 1992–2004', *Journal of Child Sexual Abuse*, 19(1): 99–117.

Church of Scotland (2013) *Social Care Council Proposed Deliverance*. Online. Available: http://www.churchofscotland.org.uk/__data/assets/pdf_file/0005/13793/6_SOCIAL_2013.pdf (accessed 28 May 2013).

CICA (2009) *Commission to Inquire into Child Abuse Investigation Committee Report*. Online. Available: http://www.childabusecommission.com/rpt/pdfs/ (accessed 11 June 2013).

Clark, J.A. (1995) 'Islamic social welfare organizations in Cairo: Islamization from below?', *Arab Studies Quarterly*, 17(4): 11–28.

Clark, J.A. (2008) 'FBOs and change in the context of authoritarianism: the Islamic Center Charity Society in Jordan', in G. Clarke and M. Jennings (eds) *Development, Civil Society and Faith-based Organizations*, Basingstoke: Palgrave Macmillan.

Clarke, G. (2008) 'Faith-based organizations and international development: an overview', in G. Clarke and M. Jennings (eds) *Development, Civil Society and Faith-based Organizations*, Basingstoke: Palgrave Macmillan.

Clarke, G. and Jennings, M. (2008) 'Introduction', in G. Clarke and M. Jennings (eds) *Development, Civil Society and Faith-based Organizations*, Basingstoke: Palgrave Macmillan.

Cnaan, R.A. and Boddie, S.C. (2002) 'Charitable Choice and faith-based welfare: a call for social work', *Social Work*, 47(3): 224–235.

Cnaan, R.A. and Boddie, S.C. (2006) 'Setting the context: assessing the effectiveness of faith-based social services', *Journal of Religion and Spirituality in Social Work*, 25(3/4): 5–18.

Cnaan, R.A. and Newman, S. (2010) 'The safety net and faith-based services', *Journal of Religion and Spirituality in Social Work*, 29(4): 321–336.

Cnaan, R.A., Wineburg, R.J. and Boddie, S.C. (1999) *The Newer Deal: Social work and religion in partnership*, New York: Colombia University Press.

Cnaan, R.A., Kang, J.J., McGrew, C.C. and Sinha, J.W. (2003) 'Identiteit meetbaar maken: gedachten van de andere kant van de Atlantische Oceaan (Incorporating religious identity into organizational identity: thoughts from the other side of the Atlantic ocean)', *Bulletib Onderwijs & Inspiratie*, 32(5): 23–25.

Coalition of Care and Support Providers in Scotland (2013) *About CCPS*. Online. Available: http://ccpscotland.org/about-ccps (accessed 27 May 2013).

Collins, S. (2008) 'Statutory social workers: stress, job satisfaction, coping, social support and individual differences', *British Journal of Social Work*, 38(6), 1173–1193.

Conradson, D. (2011) 'Values, practices and strategic divestment: Christian social service organisations in New Zealand', in C. Milligan and D. Conradson (eds) *Landscapes of Voluntarism: New spaces of health, welfare and governance*, Bristol: The Policy Press.

Constable, R. (2007) 'Catholic Social Thought and the caring professions', *Journal of Religion and Spirituality in Social Work*, 26(3): 81–100.

Cosis Brown, H. and Kershaw, S. (2008) 'The legal context for social work with lesbians and gay men in the UK: updating the educational context', *Social Work Education*, 27(2): 122–130.

Cox, D. (1995) 'Asia and the Pacific', in T.D. Watts, D. Elliott and N.S. Mayadas (eds) *International Handbook on Social Work Education*, Westport, CT: Greenwood Press.

Coyte, M.E. (2007) 'Spiritual practice by day: conversations with those who know', in M.E. Coyte, P. Gilbert and V. Nicholls (eds) *Spirituality, Values and Mental Health: Jewels for the journey*, London: Jessica Kingsley.

Cree, V.E. (1996) *Social Work: A Christian or secular discourse?*, Edinburgh: University of Edinburgh New Waverley Papers.

Cree, V.E. and Davis, A. (2007) *Social Work: Voices from the inside*, London: Routledge.

Crisp, B.R. (2010) 'Catholic agencies: making a distinct contribution to Australian social welfare provision?', *The Australasian Catholic Record*, 87(4): 440–451.

Crisp, B.R. (2012) 'The spiritual implications of sexual abuse: not an issue only for religious women', *Feminist Theology*, 20(2): 133–145.

Crisp, B.R. (2013) 'Social work and faith-based agencies in Sweden and Australia', *International Social Work*, 56(3): 343–355.

Crisp, B.R., Anderson, M.R., Orme, J. and Green Lister, P. (2005) *Knowledge Review. Learning and Teaching in Social Work Education: Textbooks and frameworks on assessment*, Bristol: The Policy Press.

Crossreach (2013a) *What We Do*. Online. Available: http://www.crossreach.org.uk/what-we-do (accessed 27 May 2013).

Crossreach (2013b) *Our Christian Ethos*. Online. Available: http://www.crossreach.org.uk/our-christian-ethos (accessed 13 June 2013).

Davie, G. (2012) 'A European perspective on religion and welfare: contrasts and commonalities', *Social Policy and Society*, 11(4): 589–599.

Davies-Kildea, J. (2007) *Faith in Action: A study of holistic models care, for highly disadvantaged people, which have been established in faith-based communities*, Brunswick, Victoria: The Salvation Army. Online. Available: http://www.salvationarmy.org.au/Global/State%20pages/Victoria/Brunswick%20Corps/faith%20in%20action%20report.pdf (accessed 25 March 2013).

Davis, D.H. (1996) 'The church-state implications of the new welfare reform law', *Journal of Church and State*, 38(4): 719–732.

Davis, F. (2009) 'Faith advocacy and the EU anti-poverty process: a case of Caritas', *Public Money and Management*, 29(6): 379–386.

Davis, F., Paulhus, E. and Bradstock, A. (2008) *Moral, But No Compass: Government, church and the future of welfare*, Chelmsford: Matthew James Publishing.

De Cordier, B. (2009) 'Faith-based aid. Globalization and the humanitarian frontline: an analysis of western-based Muslim aid organizations', *Disasters*, 33(4): 608–628.

de Leeuw, E., McNess, A., Stagnitti, K. and Crisp, B.R. (2007) *Acting at the Nexus: Integration of research, policy and practice*, Geelong, Victoria: Deakin University.

Degeneffe, C.E. (2003) 'What is Catholic about Catholic Charities?', *Social Work*, 48(3): 374–383.

DeHart, D.D. (2010) 'Collaboration between victim services and faith organizations: benefits, challenges and recommendations', *Journal of Religion and Spirituality in Social Work*, 29(4): 349–371.

Deines, H. (2008) 'The Catholic Worker Movement: communities of personal hospitality and justice', *Social Work and Christianity*, 35(4): 429–448.

Dezerotes, D. (2009) 'Religious resurgence, human survival and global religious social work', *Journal of Religion and Spirituality in Social Work*, 28(1–2): 63–81.

DiMaggio, P.J. and Powell, W.W. (1983) 'The Iron Cage revisited: institutional isomorphism and collective rationality in organizational fields', *American Sociological Review*, 48(2): 147–160.

Dinham, A. (2009) *Faiths, Public Policy and Civil Society: Problems, policies, controversies*, Basingstoke: Palgrave Macmillan.

Dinham, A. (2012a) *Faith and Social Capital After the Debt Crisis*, Basingstoke: Palgrave Macmillan.

Dinham, A. (2012b) 'The multi-faith paradigm in policy and practice: problems, challenges and directions', *Social Policy and Society*, 11(4): 577–587.

Dinham, A. and Lowndes, V. (2008) 'Religion, resources and representation: three narratives of faith engagement in British urban governance', *Urban Affairs Review*, 43(6): 817–845.

Dinham, A. and Lowndes, V. (2009) 'Faith and the public realm', in A. Dinham, R. Furbey and V. Lowndes (eds) *Faith in the Public Realm: Controversies, policies and practices*, Bristol: The Policy Press.

Dinham, A., Furbey, R. and Lowndes,V. (eds) (2009) *Faith in the Public Realm: Controversies, policies and practices*, Bristol: The Policy Press.

Eastham, M. (2002) 'Vocation and social care', in M. Nash and B. Stewart (eds) *Spirituality and Social Care: Contributing to personal and community well-being*, London: Jessica Kingsley.

Ebaugh, H.R., Chafetz, J.S. and Pipes, P.F. (2005) 'Faith-based social service organizations and government funding: data from a national survey', *Social Science Quarterly*, 86(2): 273–292.

Ebaugh, H.R., Chafetz, J.S. and Pipes, P.F. (2006) 'Where's the faith in faith-based organizations? Measures and correlates of religiosity in faith-based social service coalitions', *Social Forces*, 84(4): 2259–2272.

Ebaugh, H.R., Pipes, P.F., Chafetz, J.S. and Daniels, M. (2003) 'Where's the religion? Distinguishing faith-based from secular social service agencies', *Journal for the Scientific Study of Religion*, 42(3): 411–426.

Ebear, J., Csiernik, R. and Béchard, M. (2006) 'Is there a place for social work within the Catholic Church?', *Critical Social Work*, 7(1). Online. Available: http://www1.uwindsor.ca/criticalsocialwork/is-there-a-place-for-social-work-within-the-catholic-church (accessed 7 October 2013).

Ebear, J., Csiernik, R. and Béchard, M. (2008) 'Furthering parish wellness: including social work as part of a Catholic pastoral team', *Social Work and Christianity*, 35(2): 179–186.

Eby, J., Iverson, E., Smyers, J. and Kekic, E. (2011) 'The faith community's role in refugee resettlement in the United States', *Journal of Refugee Studies*, 24(3): 586–605.

Edgardh, N. and Pettersson, P. (2010) 'The Church of Sweden: a church for all especially the most vulnerable', in A. Bäckström, G. Davie, N. Edgardh and P. Pettersson (eds) *Welfare and Religion in 21st Century Europe: Volume 1 Configuring the connections*, Farnham: Ashgate.

Edgardh Beckman, N., Ekstrand, T. and Pettersson, P. (2006) 'The Church of Sweden as an Agent of Welfare: the Case of Gävle', in A.B. Yeung, N. Edgardh Beckman and P. Pettersson (eds) *Churches in Europe as Agents of Welfare: Sweden, Norway and Finland*, Uppsala: Institute for Diaconal and Social Studies.

Edwards, A.W. (2013) 'Parents' satisfaction, preferences, and perception of staff competence and quality of services rendered at faith-based daycare centres', *Social Work and Christianity*, 40(1): 46–70.

Ekstrand, T. (2011) 'Thinking theologically about welfare and religion', in A. Bäckström, G. Davie, N. Edgardh and P. Pettersson (eds) *Welfare and Religion in 21st Century Europe: Volume 2 Gendered religious and social change*, Farnham: Ashgate.

Ellenson, D. (2006) 'What makes a Jewish organization "Jewish"?', *Journal of Jewish Communal Service*, 81(3/4): 129–132.

Esping-Andersen, G. (1990) *The Three Worlds of Welfare Capitalism*, Cambridge: Polity Press.

Fagan, D.M., Kiger, A. and van Teijlingen, E. (2010) 'A survey of faith leaders concerning health promotion and the level of healthy living activities in faith communities in Scotland', *Global Health Promotion*, 17(4): 15–23.

Farnsley, A.E. (2001) 'Faith-based action', *The Christian Century*, 118(9): 12–15.

Ferguson, K.M. (2004) 'Shaping street-children organizations across the Americas: the influence of political, social and cultural contexts on Covenant House and Casa Alianza', *Journal of Religion and Spirituality in Social Work*, 23(4): 85–102.

Ferguson, K.M., Wu, Q., Spruijit-Metz, D. and Dryness, G. (2007) 'Outcomes evaluations in faith-based social services: are we evaluating *faith* accurately?', *Research on Social Work Practice*, 17(2): 264–276.

Ferris, E. (2005) 'Faith-based and secular humanitarian organizations', *International Review of the Red Cross*, 87(2): 311–325.

Ferris, E. (2011) 'Faith and humanitarianism: it's complicated', *Journal of Refugee Studies*, 24(3): 606–625.

Fiddian-Qasmiyeh, E. (2011) 'The pragmatics of performance: putting "faith" in aid in the Sahrawi refugee camps', *Journal of Refugee Studies*, 24(3): 533–547.

Fischer, R.L. and Stelter, J.D. (2006) 'Testing faith: improving the evidence base on faith-based human services', *Journal of Religion and Spirituality in Social Work*, 25(3/4): 5–18.

Fix, B. and Fix, E. (2002) 'From charity to client-oriented social service production: a social profile of religious welfare associations in Western European comparison', *European Journal of Social Work*, 5(1): 55–62.

Fokas, E. (2006) 'The Greek Orthodox Church as an agent of welfare: the case of Thiva and Livadeia', in A.B. Yeung, N. Edgardh Beckman and P. Pettersson (eds) *Churches in Europe as Agents of Welfare: England, Germany, France, Italy and Greece*, Uppsala: Institute for Diaconal and Social Studies.

Fouka, G., Plakas, S., Taket, A., Boudioni, M. and Dandoulakis, M. (2012) 'Health-related religious rituals of the Greek Orthodox Church: their uptake and meanings', *Journal of Nursing Management*, 20(8): 1058–1068.

Frisina, A. (2006) 'The Catholic Church in Italy as an agent of welfare: the case of Vicenza', in A.B. Yeung, N. Edgardh Beckman and P. Pettersson (eds) *Churches in Europe as Agents of Welfare: Sweden, Norway and Finland*, Uppsala: Institute for Diaconal and Social Studies.

Fulford, K.W.M. and Woodbridge, K. (2007) 'Values-based practice: help and healing within a shared theology of diversity', in M.E. Coyte, P. Gilbert and V. Nicholls (eds) *Spirituality, Values and Mental Health: Jewels for the journey*, London: Jessica Kingsley.

Furbey, R. and Macey, M. (2005) 'Religion and urban regeneration: a place for faith?', *Policy and Politics*, 33(1): 95–116.

Furbey, R., Dinham, A., Farnell, R., Finneron, D., Wilkinson, G., Howarth, C., Hussain, D. and Palmer, S. (2005) *Faith as Social Capital: Connecting or dividing?*, York: Joseph Rowntree Foundation.

Furness, S. and Gilligan, P. (2010a) *Religion, Belief and Social Work: Making a difference*, Bristol: The Policy Press.

Furness, S. and Gilligan, P. (2010b) 'Social work, religion and belief: developing a framework for practice', *British Journal of Social Work*, 40(8): 2185–2202.

Furness, S. and Gilligan, P. (2012) 'Faith-based organisations and UK welfare services: exploring some ongoing dilemmas', *Social Policy and Society*, 11(4): 601–612.

Gardner, F. (2006) *Working with Human Service Organisations: Creating connections for practice*, South Melbourne: Oxford University Press.

Gardner, F. (2011) *Critical Spirituality: A holistic approach to community practice*, Farnham: Ashgate.

Garland, D.R., Wolfer, T.A. and Myers, D.R. (2008) 'How 35 congregations launched and sustained community ministries', *Social Work and Christianity*, 35(3): 229–257.

Gatrad, A.R., Brown, E., Notta, H. and Sheikh, A. (2003) 'Palliative care needs of minorities: understanding their needs is the key', *British Medical Journal*, 327(7408): 176–177.

Gatrad, A.R. and Sheikh, A. (2002) 'Palliative care for Muslims and issues before death', *International Journal of Palliative Care Nursing*, 8(11): 526–531.

Gilligan, P. (2008) 'Child abuse and spirit possession: not just an issue for African migrants', *Childright*, 245: 28–31.

Gilligan, P. (2009) 'Considering religion and beliefs in child protection and safeguarding work: is any consensus emerging?', *Child Abuse Review*, 18(2): 94–110.

Gilligan, P. (2010) 'Faith-based approaches', in M. Gray and S. Webb (eds) *Ethics and Value Perspectives in Social Work*, Basingstoke: Palgrave Macmillan.

Gilligan, P. and Akhtar, S. (2006) 'Cultural barriers to the disclosure of sexual abuse in Asian communities: listening to what women say', *British Journal of Social Work*, 36(8): 1361–1377.

Gleeson, D.J. (2000) 'Professional social workers and welfare bureaus: the origins of Australian Catholic social work', *The Australasian Catholic Record*, 77(2): 185–202.

Gleeson, D.J. (2008a) 'Some new perspectives on early Australian social work', *Australian Social Work*, 61(3): 207–225.

Gleeson, D.J. (2008b) 'The foundation and first decade of the National Catholic Welfare Committee', *The Australasian Catholic Record*, 85(1): 15–36.

Glennon, F. (2000) 'Blessed be the ties that bind? The challenge of Charitable Choice to moral obligation', *Journal of Church and State*, 42(4): 825–843.

Göcmen, I. (2013) 'The role of faith-based organizations in social welfare systems: a comparison of France, Germany, Sweden and the United Kingdom', *Nonprofit and Voluntary Sector Quarterly*, 42(3): 495–516.

Graham, J.R., Schiff, J.W. and Coates, J. (2011) 'Introduction: social work, spirituality and social practices', *Journal of Religion and Spirituality in Social Work*, 30(3): 187–192.

Gray, A., Broadbent, J. and Lavender, M. (2009) 'Editorial: faith in themes', *Public Money and Management*, 29(6): 331.

Green, M. (2010) 'Youth workers as converters? Ethical issues in faith-based youth work', in S. Banks (ed.) *Ethical Issues in Youth Work*, 2nd edn, London: Routledge.

Griffiths, M. (2011) 'Never giving up', Province Express, 5 July 2011. Online. Available: http://www.express.org.au/article.aspx?aeid=27117 (accessed 12 March 2013).

Grønbjerg, K.A. and Nelson, S. (1998) 'Mapping small religious non-profit organizations: an Illinois profile', *Nonprofit and Voluntary Sector Quarterly*, 27(1): 13–31.

Guttmann, D. and Cohen, B-Z. (1995) 'Israel', in T.D. Watts, D. Elliott and N.S. Mayadas (eds) *International Handbook on Social Work Education*, Westport, CT: Greenwood Press.

Hansson, A-S. (2006) 'The psychosocial work environment in the Church of Sweden: an explorative study', *Nonprofit Management and Leadership*, 16(3): 329–343.

Harb, M. (2008) 'Faith-based organizations as effective development partners? Hezbollah and post-war reconstruction in Lebanon', in G. Clarke and M. Jennings (eds) *Development, Civil Society and Faith-based Organizations*, Basingstoke: Palgrave Macmillan.

Harris, M., Halfpenny, P. and Rochester, C. (2003) 'A social policy role for faith-based organizations? Lessons from the UK Jewish voluntary sector', *Journal of Social Policy*, 32(1): 93–112.

Herbert, H. and Talbot, W. (2000) *Theological Perspectives on the Medically Supervised Injecting Centre to be Operated by the Uniting Church Board for Social Responsibility*. Online. Available: http://www.sydneymsic.com/back ground-and-evaluation#Theological-perspective (accessed 26 June 2013).

Hiemstra, J.L. (2002) 'Government relations with faith-based non-profit social agencies in Alberta', *Journal of Church and State*, 44(1): 19–45.

Himchak, M.V. (2005) 'Social justice and social services within the Catholic Church', *Social Work and Christianity*, 32(3): 232–247.

Hingston, C. (2012) 'Army workers march for a different tune', *Melbourne Times Weekly*. Online. Available: http://www.melbournetimesweekly.com.au/story/ 285692/army-workers-march-for-a-different-tune/ (accessed 3 January 2013).

Holden, C. and Trembath, R. (2008) *Divine Discontent – The Brotherhood of St Laurence: A history*, North Melbourne: Australian Scholarly Publishing.

Homan, K.B. (1986) 'Vocation as the quest for authentic existence', *Career Development Quarterly*, 35(1): 14–23.

Horsburgh, M. (1988) 'Words and deeds: Christianity and social welfare', *Australian Social Work*, 41(2): 17–23.

Horstmann, A. (2011) 'Ethical dilemmas and identifications of faith-based humanitarian organizations in the Karen refugee crisis', *Journal of Refugee Studies*, 24(3): 513–532.

Hugen, B. and Venema, R. (2009) 'The difference of faith: the influence of faith in human service programs', *Journal of Religion and Spirituality in Social Work*, 28(4): 405–429.

Hussain, D. (2012) 'Social policy, cultural integration and faith: a Muslim reflection', *Social Policy and Society*, 11(4): 625–635.

Hyde, C.A. (2012) 'Ethical dilemmas in human service management: identifying and resolving the challenges', *Ethics and Social Welfare*, 6(4): 351–367.

Ivereigh, A. (2009) 'New development: faith, community organizing and migration – the case of "regularization"', *Public Money and Management*, 29(6): 351–354.

Ives, N., Sinha, J.W. and Cnaan, R. (2010) 'Who is welcoming the stranger? Exploring faith-based service provision to refugees in Philadelphia', *Journal of Religion and Spirituality in Social Work*, 29(1): 71–89.

Jawad, R. (2009) *Social Welfare and Religion in the Middle East: A Lebanese perspective*, Bristol: The Policy Press.

Jawad, R. (2012a) 'Religion, social welfare and social policy in the UK: historical, theoretical and policy perspectives', *Social Policy and Society*, 11(4): 553–564.

Jawad, R. (2012b) *Religion and Faith-based Welfare: From wellbeing to ways of being*, Bristol: The Policy Press.

Jeavons, T.H. (2004) 'Religious and faith-based organizations: do we know one when we see one?', *Nonprofit and Voluntary Sector Quarterly*, 33(1): 140–145.

Jeavons, T.H. and Cnaan, R.A. (1997) 'The formation, transitions and evolution of small religious organizations', *Nonprofit and Voluntary Sector Quarterly*, 26(4s): s62–84.

Jennings, M. (2008) 'The spirit of brotherhood: Christianity and Ujamaa in Tanzania', in G. Clarke and M. Jennings (eds) *Development, Civil Society and Faith-based Organizations*, Basingstoke: Palgrave Macmillan.

Jennings, M. and Clarke, G. (2008) 'Conclusion: faith and development – of ethnocentrism, multiculturalism and religious partitioning', in G. Clarke and M. Jennings (eds) *Development, Civil Society and Faith-based Organizations*, Basingstoke: Palgrave Macmillan.

Jeppsson Grassman, E. (2010) 'Welfare in western Europe: existing regimes and patterns of change', in A. Bäckström, G. Davie, N. Edgardh, and P. and Pettersson (eds) *Welfare and Religion in 21st Century Europe: Volume 1 Configuring the connections*, Farnham: Ashgate.

Jokela, U. (2011) 'Ruling relations of the church's social work in the Lutheran church in Finland', *Social Work and Society*, 9(11): 135–138.

Jupp, J. (2009) 'Religion, immigration and refugees', in J. Jupp (ed.) *Encyclopaedia of Religion in Australia*, Melbourne: Cambridge University Press.

Kahl, S. (2005) 'The religious roots of modern poverty policy: Catholic, Lutheran, and Reformed Protestant traditions compared', *European Journal of Sociology*, 46(1): 91–126.

Karlsson Miganti, P. (2010) 'Islamic revival and young women's negotiations on gender and racism', in S. Collins-Mayo and P. Dandelion (eds) *Religion and Youth*, Farnham: Ashgate.

Kaseman, M. and Austin, M.J. (2005) 'Building a faith-based agency: a view from the inside', *Journal of Religion and Spirituality in Social Work*, 24(3): 69–91.

Kidwai, A. and Haider, A.J. (2007) 'How different religious organizations can work constructively together', in M.E. Coyte, P. Gilbert and V. Nicholls (eds) *Spirituality, Values and Mental Health: Jewels for the journey*, London: Jessica Kingsley.

Kirmani, N. and Khan, A.A. (2008) 'Does faith matter: an examination of Islamic Relief's work with refugees and displaced persons', *Refugee Survey Quarterly*, 27(2): 41–50.

Komonchak, J. (1997) 'Mission and identity in Catholic Universities', in P.W. Carey and E.C. Muller (eds) *Theological Education in the Catholic Tradition: Contemporary challenges*, New York: Crossroad.

Kroessin, M.R and Mohamed, A.S. (2008) 'Saudi Arabian NGOs in Somalia: "Wahabi" Da'wah or humanitarian aid?', in G. Clarke and M. Jennings (eds) *Development, Civil Society and Faith-based Organizations*, Basingstoke: Palgrave Macmillan.

Kunzel, R.G. (1988) 'The professionalization of benevolence: evangelicals and social workers in the Florence Crittenton Homes, 1915–1945', *Journal of Social History*, 22(1): 21–43.

La Barbera, P.A. (1992) 'Enterprise in religious-based organizations', *Nonprofit and Voluntary Sector Quarterly*, 21(1): 51–67.

Lake, M. (2013) *Faith in Action: HammondCare*, Sydney: University of New South Wales Press.

Laming, Lord (2003) *The Victoria Climbié Inquiry: Report of an inquiry by Lord Laming*, Norwich: HMSO. Online. Available: http://www.official-documents. gov.uk/document/cm57/5730/5730.pdf (accessed 1 July 2013).

Langer, N. (2003) 'Sectarian organizations serving civic purposes', in T. Tirrito and T. Cascio (eds) *Religious Organizations in Community Services: A social work perspective*, New York: Springer Publishing.

Larson, G. and Robertson, J. (2007) 'Exploring the experiences of BSW students in Christian-based practicum settings', *Social Work and Christianity*, 34(3): 244–258.

Leis-Peters, A. (2006) 'The Protestant Church as an agent of welfare in Germany: the case of Reutlingen', in A.B. Yeung, N. Edgardh Beckman and P. Pettersson (eds) *Churches in Europe as Agents of Welfare: England, Germany, France, Italy and Greece*, Uppsala: Institute for Diaconal and Social Studies.

Leis-Peters, A. (2009) 'Majority Church and welfare in Sweden: some reflections on results from two Swedish research projects: a response to Beate Hofmann', *Christian Bioethics*, 15(2): 147–153.

Leis-Peters, A. (2010) 'The German dilemma: Protestant agents of welfare in Reutlingen', in A. Bäckström, G. Davie, N. Edgardh and P. Pettersson (eds) *Welfare and Religion in 21st Century Europe: Volume 1 Configuring the connections*, Farnham: Ashgate.

Lev, R. (2003) *Shine the Light: Sexual abuse and healing in the Jewish community*, Boston, MA: Northeastern University Press.

Linden, I. (2008) 'The language of development: what are international development agencies talking about?', in G. Clarke and M. Jennings (eds) *Development, Civil Society and Faith-based Organizations*, Basingstoke: Palgrave Macmillan.

Linzer, N. (2006) 'Spirituality and ethics in long-term care', *Journal of Religion and Spirituality in Social work*, 25(1): 87–106.

Lovat, T. (2010) 'Islam and ethics', in M. Gray and S. Webb (eds) *Ethics and Value Perspectives in Social Work*, Basingstoke: Palgrave Macmillan.

Macey, M. and Carling, A. (2011) *Ethnic, Racial and Religious Inequalities: The perils of subjectivity*, Basingstoke: Palgrave Macmillan.

Macintyre, S. (1999) *A Concise History of Australia*, Cambridge: Cambridge University Press.

Mafile'o, T. (2009) 'Pasifika social work', in M. Connelly and L. Harms (eds) *Social Work: Contexts and practice*, 2nd edn, South Melbourne: Oxford University Press.

Magnusson, A. (2006) *The Quarriers Story: A history of Quarriers*, Edinburgh: Birlinn.

Mann, R. and Horsley, P. (2012) 'My voice', *Melbourne Times Weekly*. Online. Available: http://www.melbournetimesweekly.com.au/story/285385/my-voice-rose-mann-and-philomena-horsley/ (accessed 3 January 2013).

Manow, P. and van Kersbergen, K. (2009) 'Religion and the Western welfare state: the theoretical context', in K. van Kersbergen and P. Manow (eds) *Religion, Class Coalitions and Welfare States*, New York: Cambridge University Press.

McGrew, C.C. and Cnaan, R.A. (2006) 'Finding congregations: developing conceptual clarity in the study of faith-based social services', *Journal of Religion and Spirituality in Social Work*, 25(3/4): 19–37.

McLoone-Richards, C. (2012) 'Say nothing! How pathology within Catholicism created and sustained the institutional abuse of children in 20th century Ireland', *Child Abuse Review*, 21(6): 394–404.

McTernan, O. (2003) *Violence in God's Name: Religion in an age of conflict*, London: Darton, Longman & Todd.

Melville, R. and McDonald, C. (2006) 'Faith-based organisations and contemporary welfare', *Australian Journal of Social Issues*, 41(1): 69–85.

Melville-Wiseman, J. (2013) 'Teaching through the tension: resolving religious and sexuality based schism in social work education', *International Social Work*, 56(3): 290–303.

Middlemiss, M. (2006a) 'Divided by a common language: the benefits and problems created by linguistic diversity in a comparative European project', in A.B. Yeung, N. Edgardh Beckman and P. Pettersson (eds) *Churches in Europe as Agents of Welfare: Sweden, Norway and Finland*, Uppsala: Institute for Diaconal and Social Studies.

Middlemiss, M. (2006b) 'The Anglican Church as an agent of welfare: the case of Darlington', in A.B. Yeung, N. Edgardh Beckman and P. Pettersson (eds) *Churches in Europe as Agents of Welfare: England, Germany, France, Italy and Greece*, Uppsala: Institute for Diaconal and Social Studies.

Milligan, C. and Conradson, D. (2011) 'Contemporary landscapes of welfare: the "voluntary turn"?', in C. Milligan and D. Conradson (eds) *Landscapes of Voluntarism: New spaces of health, welfare and governance*, Bristol: The Policy Press.

MSIC (2013) *Background and Evaluation*. Online. Available: http://www.sydneymsic.com/background-and-evaluation (accessed 26 June 2013).

Murphy, J. (2006) 'The other welfare state: non-government agencies and the mixed economy of welfare in Australia', *History Australia*, 3(2): 44.1–15.

Murphy, J. (2007) 'Suffering, vice and justice: religious imaginaries and welfare agencies in post-war Melbourne', *Journal of Religious History*, 31(3): 287–304.

Murray, S., Murphy, J., Branigan, E. and Malone, J. (2009) *After the Orphanage: Life beyond the children's home*, Sydney: UNSW Press.

Neagoe, A. (2013) 'Ethical dilemmas for the social work professional in a (post-) secular society, with special reference to the Christian social worker', *International Social Work*, 56(3): 310–325.

Netting, F.E. (1982) 'Secular and religious funding of church-related agencies', *Social Service Review*, 56(4): 586–604.

Netting, F.E. (1984) 'Church-related agencies and social welfare', *Social Service Review*, 58(3): 404–420.

Netting, F.E. (2004) 'Commentary on typology of religious characteristics of social service and educational organizations and programs', *Nonprofit and Voluntary Sector*, 33(1): 135–139.

Netting, F.E., O'Connor, M.K., Thomas, M.L. and Yancey, G. (2005) 'Mixing and phasing of roles among volunteers, staff, and participants in faith-based programs', *Nonprofit and Voluntary Sector Quarterly*, 34(2): 179–205.

Northern, V.M. (2009) 'Social workers in congregational contexts', *Social Work and Christianity*, 36(3): 265–285.

O'Connor, I., Wilson, J., Setterlund, D. and Hughes, M. (2008) *Social Work and Human Service Practice*, 5th edn, Frenchs Forest: Pearson Education.

Ogilvie, C. (2008) 'Succession planning and generational change II', in N. Ormerod (ed.) *Identity and Mission in Catholic Agencies*, Strathfield, NSW: St Pauls Publications.

Orji, N. (2011) 'Faith-based aid to people affected by conflict in Jos, Nigeria: an analysis of the role of Christian and Muslim organizations', *Journal of Refugee Studies*, 24(3): 473–492.

Ortiz, L.P.A. (2003) 'Religiosity and spirituality in social work: a retrospective and contemporary analysis', in T. Tirrito and T. Cascio (eds) *Religious Organizations in Community Services: A social work perspective*, New York: Springer Publishing.

Ozanne, E. and Rose, D. (2013) *The Organisational Context of Human Service Practice*, South Yarra, Victoria: Palgrave Macmillan.

Palmer, V. (2011) 'Analysing cultural proximity: Islamic Relief worldwide and Rohingya refugees in Bangladesh', *Development in Practice*, 21(1): 96–108.

Parekh, P. (2009) 'Foreword', in A. Dinham, R. Furbey and V. Lowndes (eds) *Faith in the Public Realm: Controversies, policies and practices*, Bristol: The Policy Press.

Parsitau, D.S. (2011) 'The role of faith and faith-based organizations among internally displaced persons in Kenya', *Journal of Refugee Studies*, 24(3): 493–512.

Paton, R., Ali, H. and Taylor, L. (2009) 'Government support for faith-based organizations: the case of a development programme for faith leaders', *Public Money and Management*, 29(6): 363–370.

Payne, M. (2005) *The Origins of Social Work: Continuity and change*, Basingstoke: Palgrave Macmillan.

Pessi, A.B. (2010) 'The church as a place of encounter: communality and the good life in Finland', in A. Bäckström, G. Davie, N. Edgardh and P. Pettersson (eds) *Welfare and Religion in 21st Century Europe: Volume 1 Configuring the connections*, Farnham: Ashgate.

Pettersson, P. (2011) 'Majority churches as agents of European welfare: a sociological approach', in A. Bäckström, G. Davie, N. Edgardh and P. Pettersson (eds) *Welfare and Religion in 21st Century Europe: Volume 2 Gendered religious and social change*, Farnham: Ashgate.

Phillips, I., Raske, M., Bordelon, T.D., Lautner-Uebelhor, T. and Collins, J.F. (2008) '"Catholic Charities" neighbor to neighbor: preliminary findings of a faith-based initiative', *Journal of Religion and Spirituality in Social Work*, 27(4): 361–383.

Pilgrim, D. (2011) 'The child abuse crisis in the Catholic Church: international, national and policy perspectives', *Policy and Politics*, 39(3): 309–324.

Pilgrim, D. (2012) 'Child abuse in Irish Catholic settings: a non-reductionist account', *Child Abuse Review*, 21(6): 405–413.

Pipes, P.F. and Ebaugh, H.R. (2002) 'Faith-based coalitions, social services and government funding', *Sociology of Religion*, 63(1): 49–68.

Powell, F., Geoghegan, M., Scanlon, M. and Swirak, K. (2013) 'The Irish charity myth, child abuse and human rights: contextualising the Ryan Report into care institutions', *British Journal of Social Work*, 43(1): 7–23.

Prochaska, F. (2006) *Christianity and Social Service in Modern Britain: The disinherited spirit*, Oxford: Oxford University Press.

Quadagno, J. and Rohlinger, D. (2009) 'The religious factor in U.S. welfare state politics', in K. van Kersbergen and P. Manow (eds) *Religion, Class Coalitions and Welfare States*, New York: Cambridge University Press.

Quinlan, F. (2008) 'Common challenges for health, education and social services', in N. Ormerod (ed.) *Identity and Mission in Catholic Agencies*, Strathfield, NSW: St Paul's Publications.

Ranson, D. (2008) 'A service shaped by Catholic identity', in N. Ormerod (ed.) *Identity and Mission in Catholic Agencies*, Strathfield, NSW: St Paul's Publications.

Ranson, D. (2012) *The Hospitality of Ministry: Exercising Christian ministry with a trinitarian heart*, Strathfield, NSW: St Paul's Publications.

Reid, R. (2008) 'Succession planning and generational change I', in N. Ormerod (ed.) *Identity and Mission in Catholic Agencies*, Strathfield, NSW: St Paul's Publications.

Ressler, L.E. and Hodge, D.R. (2003) 'Silenced voices: social work and the oppression of conservative narratives', *Social Thought*, 22(1): 125–142.

Ressler, L.E. and Hodge, D.R. (2005) 'Religious discrimination in social work', *Journal of Religion and Spirituality in Social Work*, 24(4): 55–74.

Rogers, R.K. (2009) 'Community collaboration: practices of effective collaboration as reported by three urban faith-based social service programs', *Social Work and Christianity*, 36(2): 326–345.

Rogers, R.K., Yancey, G. and Singletary, J. (2005) 'Methodological challenges in identifying promising and exemplary practices in urban faith-based social service programs', *Social Work and Christianity*, 32(3): 189–208.

Saedi, A.A. (2004) 'The accountability of para-governmental organizations (Bonyards): the case of Iranian foundations', *Iranian Studies*, 37(3): 479–498.

Scales, T.L. (2011) '"Accepting a trust so responsible": Christians caring for children at Buckner Orphan's Home, Dallas, Texas, 1979–1909', *Social Work and Christianity*, 38(3): 332–355.

Scales, T.L. and Kelly, M.S. (2011) '"To Give Christ to the Neighborhood": a corrective look at the Settlement Movement and early Christian social workers', *Social Work and Christianity*, 38(3): 356–376.

Schneider, J.A. (1999) 'Trusting that of God in everyone: three examples of Quaker-based social service in disadvantaged communities', *Nonprofit and Voluntary Sector Quarterly*, 28(3): 269–295.

Schneider, J.A. (2013) 'Comparing stewardship across faith-based organizations', *Nonprofit and Voluntary Sector Quarterly*, 42(3): 517–539.

Schuiringa, W. (2007) 'Helping practices within a strongly defined faith tradition', in F. Gale, N. Bolzan and D. McRae-McMahon (eds) *Spirited Practices: Spirituality and the helping professions*, Crows Nest, NSW: Allen & Unwin.

Schwartz, K.D., Warkentin, B. and Wilkinson, M. (2008) 'Faith-based social services in North America: a comparison of American and Canadian religious history and initiative', *Social Work and Christianity*, 35(2): 123–147.

Sen, R., Kendrick, A., Milligan, I. and Hawthorn, M. (2007) 'Historical abuse in residential child care in Scotland 1950–1995: a literature review', in T. Shaw, *Historical Abuse Systematic Review: Residential schools and children's homes in Scotland 1950 to 1995*, Edinburgh: Scottish Government.

Senate Community Affairs Reference Committee (2004) *Forgotten Australians: A report on Australians who experienced institutional or out-of-home care as children*, Canberra: Australian Government.

Shaw, T. (2007) *Historical Abuse Systematic Review: Residential schools and children's homes in Scotland 1950 to 1995*, Edinburgh: Scottish Government.

Shaw, T. (2011) *Time To Be Heard: A pilot forum*, Edinburgh: Scottish Government.

Sheridan, M.J., Bullis, R.K., Adcock, C.R., Berlin, S.D. and Miller, P.C. (1992) 'Practitioners' personal and professional attitudes and behavior toward religion and spirituality: issues for education and practice', *Journal of Social Work Education*, 28(2): 190–203.

Sherr, M.E. and Rogers, R.K. (2009) 'Administrative practices in religious organizations: describing fundamental practices', *Social Work and Christianity*, 36(2): 125–126.

Sherr, M.E., Rogers, R.K., Dennison, A. and Paul, D. (2009) 'Exploring the role of research in evangelical service organizations: lessons from a university/ agency partnership', *Social Work and Christianity*, 36(2): 217–229.

Sider, R.J. and Unruh, H.R. (2004) 'Typology of religious characteristics of social service and educational organizations and programs', *Nonprofit and Voluntary Sector Quarterly*, 33(1): 109–134.

Sinha, J.W. (2013) 'Unintended consequences of the faith-based initiative: organizational and religious identity within faith-based human service organizations', *Nonprofit and Voluntary Sector Quarterly*, 42(3): 563–583.

Siporin, M. (1986) 'Contribution of religious values to social work and the law', *Social Thought*, 12(4): 35–50.

Smith, G. (2002) 'Religion, and the rise of social capitalism: the faith communities in community development and urban regeneration in England', *Community Development Journal*, 37(2): 167–177.

Smith, J.M. (1989) 'Individual and organizational ethics', *Social Thought*, 15(3–4): 90–101.

Smith, K.S. and Teasley, M. (2009) 'Social work research on faith-based programs: a movement towards evidence-based practice', *Journal of Religion and Spirituality in Social Work*, 28(3): 306–327.

Smith, M. (2006) 'Act justly, love tenderly, walk humbly', *Residential Child and Youth Care Practice*, 19(4): 5–17.

Smith, M. (2008) 'Historical abuse in residential child care: an alternative view', *Practice*, 20(1): 29–41.

Smith, M. (2010) 'Victim narratives of historical abuse in residential child care: do we really know what we think we know?', *Qualitative Social Work*, 9(3): 303–320.

Smith, M., Cree, V.E. and Clapton, G. (2012) 'Time to be heard: interrogating the Scottish Government's response to historical child abuse', *Scottish Affairs*, 78: 1–24.

Smith, S. and Sosin, M. (2001) 'The varieties of faith-related agencies', *Public Administration Review*, 61(6): 651–670.

Snyder, S. (2011) 'Un/settling angels: faith-based organizations and asylum seeking in the UK', *Journal of Refugee Studies*, 24(3): 565–585.

Sosin, M.R. and Smith, S.R. (2006) 'New responsibilities of faith-related agencies', *The Policy Studies Journal*, 34(4): 533–562.

St Andrew's Children's Society (2012) *Annual Review 2011: 2012*, Edinburgh: St Andrew's Children's Society.

Stein, M. (2006) 'Missing years of abuse in children's homes', *Child and Family Social Work*, 11(1): 11–21.

Stewart, C. (2009) 'The inevitable conflict between religious and social work values', *Journal of Religion and Spirituality in Social Work*, 28(1–2): 35–47.

Svare, G.M., Hylton, M. and Albers, E. (2007) 'On our own: social workers talk about spiritually-sensitive practice within an organizational context', *Journal of Religion and Spirituality in Social Work*, 26(4): 95–113.

Swain, S. (2005) 'Do you want religion with that? Welfare history in a secular age', *History Australia*, 2(3): 79.1–8.

Swain, S. (2009) 'Welfare work and charitable organisations', in J. Jupp (ed.) *Encyclopaedia of Religion in Australia*, Melbourne: Cambridge University Press.

Swinton, J. (2007) 'Researching spirituality and mental health: a perspective from the research', in M.E. Coyte, P. Gilbert and V. Nicholls (eds) *Spirituality, Values and Mental Health: Jewels for the journey*, London: Jessica Kingsley.

Tangenberg, K.M. (2005) 'Faith-based human service initiatives: considerations for social work practice and theory', *Social Work*, 50(3): 197–206.

Taylor, P.V. (1995) 'France', in T.D. Watts, D. Elliott and N.S. Mayadas (eds) *International Handbook on Social Work Education*, Westport, CT: Greenwood Press.

Thaut, L.C. (2009) 'The role of faith in Christian faith-based humanitarian agencies: constructing the taxonomy', *Voluntas*, 20(4): 319–350.

Thyer, B.A. (2006) 'Faith-based programs and the role of empirical research', *Journal of Religion and Spirituality in Social Work*, 25(3/4): 63–82.

Thyer, B.A. and Myers, L.L. (2009) 'Religious discrimination in social work academic programs: whither social justice?', *Journal of Religion and Spirituality in Social Work*, 28(1–2): 144–160.

Tirrito, T. and Cascio, T. (eds) (2003) *Religious Organizations in Community Services: A social work perspective*, New York: Springer.

Torry, M. (2005) *Managing God's Business: Religious and faith-based organizations and their management*, Aldershot: Ashgate.

Unruh, H.R. and Sider, R.J. (2005) *Saving Souls, Serving Society: Understanding the faith factor in church-based social ministry*, New York: Oxford University Press.

Valins, O. (2011) 'The difference of voluntarism: the place of voluntary sector care homes for older Jewish people in the United Kingdom', in C. Milligan and D. Conradson (eds) *Landscapes of Voluntarism: New spaces of health, welfare and governance*, Bristol: The Policy Press.

Vanderwoerd, J. (2004) 'How faith-based social service organizations manage secular pressures associated with government funding', *Nonprofit Management and Leadership*, 14(3): 239–262.

Warner, K.D (2009) 'The farm workers and the Franciscans: reverse evangelization as social prompt for conversion', *Spiritus*, 9(1): 69–88.

White, H. (2008) '"We can give children to homosexuals and remain Catholic" says Lancaster Adoption Agency'. Online. Available: http://www.lifesitenews.com/news/archive//ldn/2008/oct/08101408 (accessed 26 June 2013).

White, S. (1997) 'Beyond retroduction? Hermeneutics, reflexivity and social work practice', *British Journal of Social Work*, 27(5): 739–753.

Whiting, R. (2008) '"No room for religion or spirituality or cooking tips": exploring practical atheism as an unspoken consensus in the development of social work values in England', *Ethics and Social Work*, 2(1): 67–83.

Williamson, S.A. (2005) 'She saw something in me: relationships between faith community volunteers and mothers leaving welfare', *Social Work and Christianity*, 32(2): 151–167.

Williamson, S.A. and Hodges, V.G. (2006) 'It kind of made me feel important', *Social Work and Christianity*, 35(2): 43–57.

Wilson, E. (2011) 'Much to be proud of, much to be done: faith-based organizations and the politics of asylum in Australia', *Journal of Refugee Studies*, 24(3): 548–564.

Wilson, R. (1997) *Bringing Them Home: Report of the national inquiry into the separation of Aboriginal and Torres Strait Islander children from their families*, Sydney: Human Rights and Equal Opportunity Commission.

Wittberg, P.A. (2013) 'Faith-based umbrella organizations: implications for religious identity', *Nonprofit and Voluntary Sector Quarterly*, 42(3): 540–562.

Wuthnow, R., Hackett, C. and Hsu, B.Y. (2004) 'The effectiveness and trustworthiness of faith-based organizations: a study of recipient's perceptions', *Journal for the Scientific Study of Religion*, 43(1): 1–17.

Yancey, G.I. and Atkinson, K.M. (2004) 'The impact of caring in faith-based social service programs: what participants say', *Social Work and Christianity*, 31(3): 254–266.

Yancey, G., Rogers, R.K., Singletary, J., Atkinson, K. and Thomas, M.L. (2004) 'Public–private partnerships: interactions between faith-based organizations and government entities', *The Social Policy Journal*, 3(4): 5–17.

Yancey, G.I., Rogers, R.K., Singletary, J. and Sherr, M. (2009) 'A national study of administrative practices in religious organizations', *Social Work and Christianity*, 36(2): 127–142.

Yeung, A.B. (2006) 'The Finnish Lutheran Church as an agent of welfare: the case of Lahti', in A.B. Yeung, N. Edgardh Beckman and P. Pettersson (eds) *Churches in Europe as Agents of Welfare: Sweden, Norway and Finland*, Uppsala: Institute for Diaconal and Social Studies.

Yeung, A.B., Edgardh Beckman, N. and Pettersson, P. (2006) 'Researching the changing European landscape of welfare and religion', in A.B. Yeung, N. Edgardh Beckman and P. Pettersson (eds) *Churches in Europe as Agents of Welfare: Sweden, Norway and Finland*, Uppsala: Institute for Diaconal and Social Studies.

INDEX